C000256351

(*L to R*) Lise, Kate, Anne, with Selma, on the beach

A Lesser Child

Karen Gershon

A Lesser Child

An Autobiography

Peter Owen • London & Chester Springs PA

PETER OWEN PUBLISHERS
73 Kenway Road London SW5 0RE
Peter Owen books are distributed in the USA by
Dufour Editions Inc. Chester Springs PA 19425–0449

Originally published in German under the title *Das Unterkind*
© 1992 Rowohlt Verlag GmbH, Reinbek bei Hamburg
First published in Great Britain 1994
© Karen Gershon 1994

The photograph on the endpapers shows (L to R)
Lise, Kate and Anne with Selma, their mother

All Rights Reserved.
No part of this publication may be reproduced in
any form without the written permission of the publishers.

ISBN 0–7206–0899–6

A catalogue record for this book is available
from the British Library

Printed and made in Great Britain

For My Family: Past, Present, Future

. . . in this great disaster of our birth
We can be happy, and forget our doom.

George Santayana

Author's Note

This is an autobiography, as truthful as I could make it; only, I was unable to write about myself in the first person. Kate was my childhood name.

For information concerning other people and public events, I am indebted to the volumes on local history published by the town of Bielefeld.

KG

A Lesser Child

One

In earliest childhood she was never alone. Lise was little more than one year older and Anne was one year older than she. In Kate's first memories of the three of them, they are always dressed alike and she is hastening, physically or metaphorically, to catch up with her sisters. That this was impossible must have convinced her that she was a lesser child even before the Nazis came to power, when she was in her tenth year.

There was nothing in Anne's physique to betray that she was programmed for an early death. She looked perfect from birth and thrived, a sturdy girl with the colouring of a fairytale princess: hair as black as ebony, skin as white as snow; her eyes were the colour of blue flowers growing wild. She was self-seeking, would not let herself be commanded, did not need other people, and Kate she needed least of all.

Lise, coming in every way second to Anne, nevertheless was the one who inherited from the mother a distinct musical talent, and from the father, orientally brown eyes. She gave up the privilege of being Anne's lieutenant in order to colonize Kate; she did it with love and with self-sacrifice. Kate without Lise was like land without water; circumstances forced her to do without Lise as well as without Anne for most of her life.

For much, even most of each day, they were looked after by nursemaids, a succession of peasant girls straight from school, who for a year or so were willing to work for pocket-money while being trained. They were not allowed to use physical punishment; instead, they frightened. 'The gypsies will come to take you away,' they said. They threatened the three small Jews with the hellfire of Christianity. In an apposite thunderstorm they told Anne, 'You've made God angry.' It awed Kate to hear that Anne was on such personal terms with God but did not surprise her. Anne would bribe her with, 'Tidy my toys and Papa will come,' for instance, and her prophecies always came true.

In those days, Kate was content to be herself; she did not want to be Anne once she had understood that in that case she would not have had her. In the Grimm's stories to which she was addicted, it was often the third and youngest child for whom things turned out best in the end; this prompted her to invent epilogues, in which she abdicated her luck in favour of Anne. And in truth, when the time came she would willingly have died in her stead.

To deserve Anne needed a constant effort; Lise was one who could be taken for granted. She was the favourite of all the nursemaids, not only because she gave less trouble but also because of the way she looked after her little sister. Yet she deceived them: claimed responsibility for the wet patch on the carpet so that she and not Kate would be made to stand in the corner. She could not bear to see Kate made unhappy.

The flat was small but the nursemaid slept in, sharing a room with the fat-chested cook who took Kate into her bed when the child needed comforting and her mother was out, at the theatre probably, with the father. Paul and Selma made a stunning pair, he more than six foot tall and she petite; before their marriage they had both had many admirers. Still in his twenties, he was already grey-haired, after serving for four years in the German trenches on the Western Front. What this had done to him did not otherwise show; his dark eyes were merry, he had a boundless zest for life. Born not far from Berlin, he had qualified as an architect in the summer before the war.

Selma's great-grandfather had as a boy come from Galicia, founding a many-branched family, most members of which grew rich – and lost their money in the inflation which coincided with the years in which the three sisters were born. Selma's father, the girls' Opa, still observed many traditional Jewish customs, among them the one of offering Friday night hospitality to passing strangers. Thus one Friday evening in the last spring of the war he had brought home the handsome guardsman, in town recuperating from a thigh wound and determined to kiss as many pretty girls as possible before returning to the all-male world of carnage.

Selma enchanted him. She was, as the daughter of its president, the princess of the local Jewish community, with all the physical and spiritual attributes needed to grace her position. Paul saw her as beyond his reach. And she, mistaking his bashfulness for indifference, set herself the task of adding him to her conquests. He left the house with the invitation to come back the very next day, to see the Sabbath out with the family, and then to hear her play the piano and sing.

She played as well as many a professional; her voice was warm and dark. Paul did his best to conceal that he was tone-deaf and to keep his eyes away from her breasts. Selma had bidden her parents to leave them alone. She thought it a game, to make the young man want to kiss her. That was all she wanted: that compliment, a tribute to her pride. But Paul, after all he had been through, refused to abide by the rules of her social set. The little encouragement he got from her made him bold, made him unstoppable. He not only kissed her but held her close enough to let her feel that he wanted more.

No one had ever held her like that. To some extent ignorant of the facts of life – though she was in her mid-twenties – it aroused not her body but her emotions. 'Go, you must go,' she whispered. But, seeing him to the door, she told him to call again, to call again soon. As he limped past under the drawing-room window, he could hear her again playing the piano, now with a passion which he believed to be part of the music.

Her parents encouraged the soldier, partly out of patriotism, but chiefly because they always did what they could to let their only child have what she wanted. And also because so far she had rejected every eligible young man. They did not know – he did not know either, nor did she – that she loved not Paul so much as what his touch did to her sensibilities. It was not Paul but her fantasy version of him whose fiancée she became before he returned to the front.

'Show us his letters, do!' her circle of girlfriends clamoured. But she wouldn't, because his letters were unromantic. In fact, he did not write often; pride drove her to invent both letters and contents. But his photograph she showed to all callers; it made the women envy her and the young men who had courted her lose heart.

All through August she waited in vain for a letter from him. The one that eventually came failed to mention that he had been buried when a dug-out collapsed, and not been rescued until the fifth day.

Two months later, when the war was over, he returned to settle in Bielefeld, having accepted her parents' condition not to take Selma away from them. Many of his comrades from the trenches, who had also been hospitalized in this small industrial town in the Teutoburger Wald, returned there to marry, and remained his friends even when they became functionaries in the Nazi party.

When Selma and Paul walked arm in arm from under the wedding canopy down the synagogue aisle, she heard people whisper, 'There goes that guardsman with his beautiful doll.' It amazed Kate even as a child that her mother should have regarded this as a compliment. Maybe she cherished the memory of it as proof that she really had once been the best-looking Jewish girl in town, as she liked to believe.

The flat in Roland Street where their three daughters were born on the kitchen table – home confinements then being safer than those in hospital – was their second home. They started married life in two furnished rooms in a superior part of the town, where the streets were wide and tree-lined and you were only a few minutes' walk away from the forest. This was intended to give them time to find a house which Selma's father would buy for them. But before they could make their choice, prices rose; it was the beginning of the inflation. It made Selma's father and her husband – both lacking the money-sense ascribed to Jews – hesitate to buy, until it was too late.

Selma had lied about Paul while they had been engaged, bought chocolates and flowers so as to have something to show to her girlfriends when they asked her, 'What presents did he bring you?' He was not ungenerous, just poor, and he knew that her parents provided her with all, with more than she needed. It was worse when she invited her girlfriends round to show her husband off: he did what he thought of as making himself agreeable; to her it looked like flirting.

He rented an office near the centre of town; he called it modest but to her it looked mean. Visiting there she could not feel proud of him.

16

When her father asked him how things were going, instead of answering he commented on the state of the German economy; it sounded to her as if he were making excuses. He was out all day. Not wanting to leave her alone in the evenings as well, he brought his wartime comrades back with him. She found them loud and vulgar. Their company made him loud and vulgar too. And afterwards their rooms reeked of beer and tobacco. But the worst thing was having sex when they were at odds.

The landlady had refused to allow her to bring her piano. Very soon she was glad to have a respectable excuse to escape to her parents' house often. They had moved to Brackwede, then a village close to Bielefeld. 'I'm home!' she would call out as she let herself in. Her mother chided her for this but did it gently. Her mother was even smaller than she, with the same soft round face, neat eyebrows over mild blue eyes, and sensitive mouth growing melancholy with age.

One generation closer to the immigrants from Poland who made good, the mother knew Yiddish while the daughter knew French, cooked the Polish way instead of cordon bleu. She still wore a *sheitl* (wig worn by orthodox Jewish married women) as unquestioningly as her husband daily laid *tephillin* (phylacteries). As she saw things, Paul might – God forbid! – find Selma wanting, even divorce her; but unless or until he did, Selma belonged to him body and soul as Sarah had belonged to Abraham. That he was not interested in music or in literature – what did that matter compared with the fact that he did not believe in God? And had they not decided that even that did not matter because he was a good man and the one whom Selma loved?

'I didn't know that it would be like this!' Selma wailed and her mother hushed her: one must not question one's fate. Besides, she must think of the baby.

To her daughters, Selma always referred to this time as, 'When I was expecting Anne'. She was not telling the truth, which gave what she said an aura of unreality. It did not matter to Kate: she at least was still too little to be much interested in anything that had happened to her mother before she was born.

They lived in Roland Street for almost ten years. Theirs was the garden flat of a six-family house in a neighbourhood where the children played in the street but most people had more than one servant. The windows were heavily curtained for privacy, and the rooms were made small by large, solid pieces of furniture bought with a future, more spacious home in mind.

Nearby was the nicest of the town's many parks, not especially meant for children, who in those days were less catered for. This was where the three sisters were taken, weather permitting, by their nursemaid, on the way there and back two held by the hand and one on a lead. The one on the lead was mostly Lise, because Anne saw it as an indignity and Kate, always copying Anne, would argue until, to save her getting into trouble, Lise would volunteer.

There was – there still is – a lake, not small to small children, with an island providing a wooden shelter for the ducks and drakes, though not big enough for the swans.

When the grass was dry they rolled down the sloping lawns; they played hide-and-seek and running games among the flowering shrubs.

Then it was called the Bürgerpark, *bürger* meaning citizen. Later it became the Adolf Hitler Park, and Jews were forbidden to enter.

In the summer of Kate's third birthday, and again the following year, the family went for a fortnight's holiday to Scharbeutz, near Swinemünde on the Baltic coast. Their boarding-house failed to provide a cot; Kate fell out of bed on to a sheepskin rug and liked the feel of it so well that she stayed where she was until morning. The following night, she fell out of bed on purpose, in spite of the shoring up the adults had done with a pillow under the edge of the mattress, and the back of a chair to simulate cot bars. Selma, who understood her well enough to get the truth out of her on most occasions, promised that if she learned not to fall out, on their return home she would buy her a sheepskin rug.

But she didn't. What she bought was a brown and white goatskin, harsh-haired. As neither of Kate's sisters had a bedside rug, she cherished it as part of her individuality, but it was also a constant reminder that not even her mother could be relied upon.

Both fortnights were holidays for the children also in the sense that it was their mother who looked after them, more patiently and allowing

18

them more freedom than did the maids. She might have been happier looking after them always, if convention had not dictated otherwise. The years of marriage had made her grow matronly. Covered from neck to knees in the beach garments of those days, a kerchief on her head and with a parasol, she spent her leisure sitting in a deckchair reading classical novels; she did not know how to play. Paul, also already beginning to look as if he had never been young, was still almost a stranger to his daughters. In his dealings with them, he made allowances for the difference in their ages, but not for their differing personalities.

He looked – as yet he did no more than look – at other, younger women; it made Selma gather their daughters about her as a shield.

Paul had become a keen photographer and he invariably photographed the three girls together. He took a picture of their bare bottoms in a row as they piddled on the sand, which for years he carried in his wallet, to show among men. 'A photograph of my daughters?' and out it would come. Such was his sense of humour.

It was a flat beach of golden sand stretching for miles, and for a long way out the water was shallow. After days and days of the indignity of being lumped with her two little sisters, Anne rebelled, one evening when she was told that it was time to go back to the boarding-house because Kate was tired. Having got dressed, she walked into the sea, towards the setting sun, along the golden beam it had laid upon the calm water. Selma's back was turned; she was busy dressing Kate. Paul's back was turned; he was looking at other women. When they looked, Anne had disappeared almost up to her shoulders. Kate saw her.

A stranger sprang in, fully clothed, to bring her back.

The girls were rarely punished by their parents, and always only for little things, when they might need to be made to understand that they had done wrong. On that occasion, Anne was not even scolded. But she never regretted anything she had done, or if she did, she kept this to herself.

Kate was not only even littler than Lise but less gifted than she: Lise could sing. When their mother sang to them the traditional German ballads she encouraged Lise to join in, though she rarely knew all the words. Kate knew them, but because her voice was not as pleasing and she could not sing in tune, she was told to keep quiet.

When Anne put her in her place she was grateful to Anne for taking notice of her. But she could not bear not to be the equal of Lise. She needed, after being made to listen, to be the one whom the others would listen to. And so, for their favourite ballad, she made up an additional stanza, which no one but she could sing because she alone knew the words. She must then have been between four and five. More than she wanted to be congratulated, she wanted her words to be taken seriously, and so she pretended to have heard them somewhere. They believed her; her mother searched for them in her copy of Heine's poems.

It comforted Kate, the knowledge that there was more to her than people thought. It was to be an essential armour for her in the years ahead.

Because Kate's birthday fell towards the end of the summer school holidays, she was made to wait an extra year before being allowed to go to school with her sisters. Long before then she sat copying Anne doing her homework. Anne was a perfectionist. Out came the page if there was a mistake on it, and when too many pages had been torn out – and the corresponding ones at the back removed to stop it from showing – she would take a new exercise book, the old one going into the waste-paper basket. From where Kate would rescue it. Anything discarded by Anne was treasure to her.

She needed the unused pages. So powerful was the impulse in her to make up stories that she did it even before she could write, with drawings. The protagonist of her first book was a butterfly, caught by a boy with a net, tortured and killed and buried under a cross. Of course she knew how to draw a Star of David; she also knew that it was alien to her native environment.

When the girls were in their teens, their mother took to saying that in Anne she had someone with whom to discuss her problems, that Lise was a comfort to her, and that Kate was for cuddling – a role which Kate thought belittling and did not want. In one of her earliest memories, she is stealing away, boots in hand, from the bed in which her mother is sleeping, back to her sisters, too old to be expected to sleep after lunch.

Lise was the one who could not bear to be parted from their mother. More often than not, when Selma, about to go out with Paul to the theatre or to visit friends, said good night and goodbye to her daughters, Lise's nose started to bleed, and would not stop until Selma took off her evening gown and jewellery and showed herself to her wearing a housecoat and slippers. When Selma needed to stay in hospital, with blood-poisoning from a cut in her armpit, when her daughters visited her and it was time for them to leave, Lise got such a nosebleed that she was allowed to stay; a cot was put up for her right next to Selma's bed.

Lise chose for herself the role of Cinderella. She was not that when she was little, on the contrary. 'You ask,' Anne and Kate would say to her when they all three wanted something. Coming from her who was always so good, a request was more likely to be granted. It became a ritual, her nightly chant when all three were in bed, after their mother's final good night, 'Put the light on in the corridor, leave the sitting-room door ajar, switch on the wireless!'

Kate's urge to catch up with her sisters conditioned her for life to be impatient, not so much to do things as to prove that she could do them. She agitated to be allowed to leave home every school-day morning as they did, not yet consciously wanting to get away from her mother but for the sake of getting hold of a bit of existence not tempered for her by Lise. And so, at the age of five, she was put in a kindergarten, the most progressive in town, twenty-five minutes' walk for her legs from where they lived.

Neither Anne nor Lise had attended a kindergarten; for once, at last, Kate was able to think of herself as being the first. She was still so much the centre of her own universe that it came to her as a tremendous shock to find herself one of thirty or so children, and not mattering more than any other, either to the other children or to the staff. This was not how she had imagined it. She hated it and wanted to stay at home.

Her mother cajoled her; Kate could never have been got to admit it but, as far as she was concerned, her mother was and remained always right. She got used to the kindergarten, she learned to enjoy herself there. She began to belong. She secured a surrogate Lise, a best friend. She developed a childish affection for one of the staff, a pug-faced, lanky young woman of whom – Kate rightly or wrongly believed – she became the favourite.

Kate was, naturally, always put to bed first. She was meant to be asleep by the time Lise came to bed, and they were both meant to be asleep by the time Anne came. But once Kate had started at the kindergarten, instead of this making her more tired it kept her awake because it gave her such a lot to think about.

One evening, when Anne discovered that she was still awake, she asked her what the kindergarten was like. Kate thought about it: to keep Anne listening, she must make it sound perhaps more interesting than it was. There had that morning been a slight disagreement between Bärbel, the teacher she liked so much, and another teacher called Hilde. Kate dramatized this into a full-blown quarrel, which ended with Bärbel ordering Hilde about. But then Kate, identifying with Bärbel, regretted having cast her in an Anne-like role. 'No, no,' she interrupted herself, 'let me make a fresh start, it's better the other way round.'

While she was thinking about it, Anne asked, 'You mean you made all that up?' There was such amazement, such accolade in her tone of voice, that Kate became hooked for life on the telling of stories.

Two

Selma's parents were the only Opa and Oma the girls knew. Paul's mother died before Anne was born; she was named in her memory. By the time of the family's first holiday in Scharbeutz, his father must also have been dead or they would surely have gone to visit him on his estate north-east of Berlin, where he bred horses. There had been Loewenthals in Eberswalde at the time of the Black Death, assimilated enough even then not to have been driven out.

Adolf Schönfeld was a small, spare man; he wore a gold-rimmed pince-nez and by the time he became a grandfather he was totally bald. Soft-spoken and unassuming, he had learning and personality enough to have been elected president of the Jewish community in spite of not being a local man; the family had come from Aschaffenburg, south-east of Frankfurt-on-Main, when Selma was two years old.

By local standards he was an orthodox Jew. He would not eat at his daughter's table once Paul, the atheist, had teased her out of keeping a kosher home. But while her father lived she still lit Friday night candles. He filled his granddaughters' lives with all the traditional Jewish household observances; he made the sound of Hebrew familiar to them. He took them with him to the synagogue, first Anne, as soon as she was old enough to be left with the other girls. Though the community was liberal enough to have an organ, men and women and boys and girls all sat separately. Lise, who could be relied upon to be good, was taken when she was even younger and Kate, with the other two to look after her, younger still.

He taught his granddaughters by means of telling them stories, especially of the heroes of ancient times, Judah the Maccabee and Bar Kokhba, for instance, speaking of them as if he himself had

23

known them, and as if there were no difference between them and, say, the Siegfried of legend or the Friedrich of history, who were part of the girls' everyday life if only as street names. The Judaism which he taught was a fortress; to live within it was a privilege. That there was a time when Kate failed to see it like that was due to her nature, which made her believe that what was within her reach was not worth having.

The inflation had left him poor only relatively, in his own and his family's eyes, in view of the wealth he had lost. He remained the sales manager of the cement works he used to own; he still went about in a chauffeur-driven limousine, in the days when people stood still at the sight of a passing car. He had also needed to sell his house. The one he now rented in Brackwede stood above the village, one of a row of new semi-detached houses with large gardens in a private road. It had central heating and double windows, and wide sliding doors between the reception rooms large enough to hold all the local Jewish dignitaries when he invited them to help him give thanks to God for having survived the operation to remove his stomach cancer.

It was Oma who died first, when Kate was seven, and there was some mystery about her death. Perhaps the nursing home she went to was one for the mentally ill; perhaps it was true – as Kate was told many years later – that she jumped out of a window to her death.

When their Opa brought the news to Roland Street, it was late afternoon and everyone was at home. Even Anne was told to let him be, to go to the nursery. She was his favourite, and before long he came to find her. The sight of the three little mortals made him whoop with grief. He sat down on one of the low nursery chairs, covered his face with his hands, and continued to make a sound akin to laughter. His granddaughters stood before him in a row, their reactions dictated by more than their ages. Kate resented being perplexed; Lise felt miserable in empathy; Anne thought, if life is so cruel it will be cruel to me.

For the sake of their Opa, they moved out to Brackwede, into the house next door but one to his, which happened to be to let. This was in the summer of 1930, when Bielefeld was putting out its first anti-Semitic newspaper.

Now Anne was given a room of her own, emphasizing her separateness from the other two, who were not allowed to set foot in it without her permission. Lise and Kate continued to share and would not have wanted to do otherwise: they strove to think of themselves as twins, and inseparable. Sometimes they invited Anne to join in. On that first morning in the new house, for instance, when they got up at dawn to explore, it having been dark on their arrival the previous evening. Things done together with Anne were royal occasions.

The garden, all in front of the house, was longer than it was wide and sloped a little. No one had looked after it for so long that the lawn was like a meadow and running to seed. It was bordered by a thicket of shrubs. At the back of the house was a brick-walled courtyard. Beyond it, on higher ground, were a few other houses and their gardens; beyond these lay the natural forest. For the three town children, it was as if they had been transplanted into storyland.

Always, when Anne joined in, it was on the understanding that she would be in command. After this, before consenting to do anything together with the other two they would have to pass muster, because of what happened that morning. She was then nine years old and had made herself neat – would not have shown herself otherwise. Lise and Kate were not yet able to plait their hair – they had not even bothered to comb it, or to do up all their buttons. Their mother, hearing them skylarking in the garden, looked out and called them indoors. It was one of the few occasions when her understanding failed them.

'What will the neighbours think of us!' she scolded them.

'That's what comes of mixing with you,' Anne said. Lise was proud of both her sisters; Kate was proud only of Anne; Anne, for most of the time, was not proud of either.

They all three went to the village school. For Kate it was only her second term. Having heard Anne and Lise learning to read from the same primer, when her turn came she knew it all by heart; it left her with no incentive to heed the teaching. One day when she was called upon in class, she did not know where to start, dreamer that she was, though her neighbour showed her the page, because she could not relate the text in her head to the pictures. That day after school, she found Anne waiting for her. Anne did not usually wait for her sisters – if she met them by chance she refused to acknowledge them – in case others with whom she might wish to walk objected to their company, if only because they were younger.

She told Kate, 'Your teacher says that you are a dunce. How do you think that made me feel!'

So as not to shame Anne, Kate strove until, like her, she was top of her class. One day, the following year, after an arithmetic test, she discovered that she was not the only one to have got all the answers right. The other was a ragged brown boy, much too disreputable-looking to have caught her attention before. He had brown, curly hair and mischievous brown eyes. His name was Günther. After class, he bumped into her in the doorway and grinned at her. When school was out she found him waiting for her. 'I have a magpie I've taught to talk,' he told her. 'If you like, I'll show it to you.'

In her excitement, she forgot about Lise, responsible for seeing her across the main road.

Günther lived on a farm, which was perhaps not as neglected as Kate thought, but seeing it through her mother's eyes, everything looked, like the boy himself, in need of being scrubbed and tidied. The magpie couldn't really talk and was in a makeshift cage. But Günther also had rabbits – or he said they were his and Kate did not want to doubt him, she liked him too well. She liked him better than her mother would have done, not only for his sake but also for her own: to assert her autonomy. She liked him so much that she wanted to stay with him.

The rabbits were white, with pink eyes. He let her stroke them; he picked one up and put it in her arms. She had never before touched living fur and had expected it to be fastened down as on toys. The feel of it, loose over the knobbly bones, left her abashed, not so much at her ignorance as at the miracle of life.

Only the need to pee – and her inculcated inhibition about it – eventually made her go home, where a row awaited her because Lise, unable to find her after school, had come back white-faced and trembling.

Kate had no secrets from Lise and Lise had no secrets from their mother. Kate had not realized it until that day – she had believed their mother to be omniscient. Something like an emotional umbilical cord between her and Lise existed until they were separated in their teens. Kate needed to go on telling her everything. From then on she often made Lise promise to keep something a secret from their mother, not caring about the dilemma this put her in. It was as if she understood – though she didn't – that Lise never minded suffering for her sake. On the contrary, Lise welcomed it because it proved that she loved her little sister better than herself – as was her ambition.

Selma told Kate that she must not be friends with Günther. She must not go off by herself with any little boy, and especially not with 'a boy like that'. This definition of him was the only part Kate was able to understand.

Nevertheless, or perhaps because of it, she found herself a ragged brown girl, whom she took home while Selma was out and loaded with toys, for herself and her brothers and sisters; the girl's mother came to enquire if they were meant to keep them. In the meantime, Kate had had regrets: some of the toys the girl herself had chosen and Kate had not known how to stop her. She explained this. 'You can't ask for them back,' her mother said, to teach her a lesson.

More ragged and browner were the gypsy children who came every summer with the fair. They stayed for long enough to go to school and were usually put with younger children. Kate understood that this did not necessarily mean that they were backward – they missed a lot of schooling but knew more than she. She thought them romantic and wished for a life like theirs; she told herself stories about running away with them. Once, on a class outing through the fields, one of them made her a present of a cornflower. 'As blue as your eyes,' he said. She liked to believe that her eyes were cat-green, though they were in fact grey.

For a whole year, she was impatient for the time when he would come back. If he did, she was unable to recognize him, though she hung about by the gaudy caravans, with their unimaginable Romany life attracting her far more than anything at the fair.

One Sunday afternoon, the girls were all three in the sitting-room while their parents were sleeping, their mother upstairs in her bed and their father on the couch in the room next to them. They were having to be extra quiet. The two servants were out, visiting family or friends.

It may have been winter because it began to grow dark, and still their father was sleeping. Their mother had got up and was taking a bath: they could hear the water running. They could hear it running for a long time, and it went on running.

Lise and Kate stopped cutting out paper clothes for their cardboard dolls and asked Anne to listen; the house could have burned down about her while she was reading. 'Perhaps it's raining,' she said without looking up. Kate went to the window to make sure that it wasn't. 'It can't have been running for as long as you think,' Anne said. 'If the bath overflowed the water would come through the ceiling.' They all looked up and there was no sign of it. 'Switch the light on,' she told them, which they both ran to do – it was a favour to them when she asked them to do her a favour.

Anne picked up her book but she listened instead of reading. After a while, which may not have been as long as it seemed, she said, 'One of us ought to go up and see.' When there was something any one of them could do but none of them wanted to do it, it was always done by Lise. White-faced and trembling, Lise went upstairs.

'I can't make Mutti hear,' she reported. Had she really, *really* knocked? Anne asked. Was the water running through under the door – had she looked? She had and it wasn't.

They had hoped that their father would wake up, or that he would be woken by the sound of the water. They continued to wait, until that became worse than the prospect of waking him. Kate volunteered to do it but knew that the others were right when they said that he would refuse to take her seriously. Anne ruled that the correct thing was for her to do it – but he would assume that she was waking him for her own purpose and get cross. (Paul's temper was easily aroused and slow to abate.) Only if Lise were the one to wake him would he know at once that the reason for doing so was neither frivolous nor selfish. 'Tell him I told you to wake him,' Anne said to her.

As she came back they heard him springing up the stairs. Selma had locked herself in; they heard his fists banging on the door, his shouts and pleas. Afterwards they were told that he had forced the door open and, retrospectively, Kate's memory matched the deed to the noise, though at the time she did not know what it was. It did not even occur to them – such was their upbringing – to go and look. They remained where they were, probably going on with what they had been doing before the continuing sound of the water had stopped them.

Later, their father called them upstairs. 'Mutti fainted, I found her lying on the floor,' he told them. She had asked to see them but they must behave themselves. Did they ever not behave themselves in his presence? He was not awesome, but in those days he was still almost a stranger to them.

Their mother was lying flat on her back without a pillow and even her lips were white. She held out her hand to them but there was no strength in it. She looked at them one after another as if counting them, and then closed her eyes. They had been brimful of tears which the lids squeezed out.

Even Anne was not allowed to go into the forest alone – not that she would have wanted to. Her interests were sedentary: reading above all, and playing chess with their Opa. During their first year in Brackwede, they still had a nursemaid, Liesbeth, who had already been with them in Roland Street.

She was still in her teens, and more like an older cousin than a servant. She shared the girls' life but they did not share hers; on her free evenings she let down her dark blond hair and went off to activities inspired by Jesus. Liesbeth was a Lutheran, and more reticent about her faith than the Catholic housemaid, who on her return from Sunday school showed off picture cards in riotous colours made otherworldly with gold, illustrating true stories (she said), and Lise and Kate were still at the stage of believing what adults told them. They looked at the images of the crucified man and believed that what had happened to him was more terrible and more potent than any other suffering in the world and that, somehow, they too were responsible for it.

Their Opa's God was too awesome to be asked for trivial things, and in the light of what he had told them of Jewish history, everything they might have asked for was trivial. In fact, they prayed only when they went to the synagogue, and then they made use of the set Hebrew prayers, without understanding what they were saying except in a general way. They praised God for having created the world and agreed with him that it was good as it was.

'I don't think so,' Anne said and, tempering her criticism to her sisters' understanding, asked, 'Is it good for instance that Mutti has varicose veins?' Lise, who had once dislocated her best doll's arms in her attempt to put its hands together in prayer, tried to argue with her; but Anne could out-argue even the adults. If God was not attending to every detail, it meant that he was not everywhere, knowing everything. And if people who said so were wrong about that, she wanted to know what else they were wrong about before believing anything they said.

Kate, perhaps to compensate for her size, could never get enough of anything. If to believe in God was good, she reasoned, to believe also in his son must be better. To her this seemed apparent: those who did, instead of dying for ever went to heaven, and meanwhile they had the gentle Jesus as their friend, had a share in the Christmas baby and, going only a little further, could also have the Virgin Mary and have all their sins forgiven. They could join in the singing of hymns at school, and attend the scripture lessons – both having for her the allure of the forbidden.

Even before Hitler came to power, she craved to belong to the privileged majority.

School started at eight and finished at one o'clock. On Wednesday afternoons there was a Bible class in the village, held by sisters of a Protestant nursing order who wore habits like those of nuns. Having made friends with a girl who attended, Kate went there with her, and on the threshold asked if she might come in. The room was one which was used in the mornings by a nursery group; the chairs and tables were low, the holy pictures all round the wall babyish. Kate liked this, as she liked pap-food when she wasn't well.

They treated her as a visitor of importance, allowing her to choose where to sit and whether or not to join in. The book *Heidi* was being read, in instalments. Did she know it? they asked her, and because she didn't, the children vied with each other to tell her the story so far

– as if she were someone who mattered to each of them. Never had people made her feel so wanted, never had she encountered a group to which she had wanted so much to belong. After the story, she was asked to suggest a hymn. She named one the tune of which was familiar to her from school; she was given a card with the words and encouraged to join in the singing.

'Did you enjoy yourself?' they enquired when the class was over. The question was not a formality, they really wanted to know. 'Come again,' they said. 'We hope that you'll come again. Jesus hopes it.'

All week she thought about Jesus waiting for her. Besides, they also gave out pictures in which the holy had golden haloes; they had promised her that the next time she came she would be given one, too.

Even without her bringing those pictures home, they would soon have discovered there what she had been up to. 'Knowledge itself does no harm,' her Opa said when her mother consulted him. He made an opportunity to tell Kate, 'Jesus was a Jew. Mary and Joseph were Jewish.'

She knew that he would not lie to her but she did not believe him.

The year 1931 must have been a good one for Paul professionally. He moved his office to larger, more centrally situated premises, engaged a second apprentice and also a secretary – too pretty for Selma's peace of mind. There was money enough for his daughters to get for Hanukkah all they had wished for, including bicycles. Anne liked to keep her possessions immaculate. She was also unsporting: Anne taking her bicycle for a walk – which was what she did with it – became a family joke.

Liesbeth, too, was given a bicycle, although she was leaving to join a Lutheran nursing order. Selma did not replace her, but arranged for a young woman to come in the early afternoon, whenever the weather was suitable, to take the girls for a walk. After this arrangement broke down, Lise and Kate began to run wild.

They had their rituals. For instance, in the spring, when their sandbox was refilled, they decorated it with leaves and flowers, the ceremony growing more elaborate every year. But its climax remained Anne coming to have a look and pronouncing it good. In the autumn they, like other children, flew their kites on the hillside, running over sloping fields of stubble. They spent more time exploring secret places, their imagination feeding on what they did not understand – a long stretch of high wall deep in the forest, for instance, seemingly closing off nothing except more trees. They strove to empathize with whatever lived wild, liking best what gave their thoughts most scope: migrant birds, also tadpoles and caterpillars because they had the power to transform themselves. Not till they left this Eden did Kate begin to outgrow the books presenting creatures and things as if they were human.

Selma, as a girl, had owned a greyhound, from when he was a puppy until, at the age of twelve, he needed to be put down. His death had caused her so much grief that she had resolved never to own another pet – or perhaps this was what she told her daughters because she did not want to have an animal in the house. They knew that, on the whole, they were lucky in having the mother they had. The girl next door, Sieglinde, was allowed to play with her best doll only on Sundays, and then was not allowed to bring it out. She was forbidden to bounce her ball against the house wall. (Anne chose not to do so with hers so as not to spoil it; their mother did not make rules about their things.) But even Sieglinde, or rather her mother, kept rabbits in hutches, which stood in the courtyard.

Their Opa had for a while owned a dog, a boxer, when their Oma had still been alive. Once, coming on a visit from Roland Street, after the housekeeper had opened the door, Kate the impatient had heedlessly run past her to the room in which she knew her grandparents to be. But before she could reach them, the newly acquired dog had sprung at her and placed its paws on her shoulders, their heads now at the same height. The fright this gave her resulted in jaundice. Nevertheless – such was her need to be a Lise to something – in her ninth year she made friends with a grey wire-haired dog, part terrier, waiting for his master outside a house which she passed on her way home from school.

On the second occasion, after she had talked to and stroked him, he got up and followed her for a little way. Every time he followed her a little further until, without coercion, though she did not discourage him either, he came with her all the way home. 'He's chosen me to look after him,' she said. He must be lost or he must have been abandoned, she argued, believing it because she wanted it so: she needed to see whomsoever she loved as, somehow, a victim. She named him Tasso.

Possibly Selma left it to Paul to notify the police and he, in his careless way, forgot about it; a few days passed before the owner came and called them thieves. Kate was made to explain and to apologize. Afterwards, her mother said to her, 'As Jews, we cannot afford to lay ourselves open to criticism, let alone accusations.'

Hitler was not yet in power but the Nazis and their ideas were gaining increasing support.

Three

Three years after his wife's death, at the age of sixty-three, Adolf Schönfeld remarried. His new wife was young – not much older than Selma – with a couple of teenaged children who spoke only French. She was the widow of a Frenchman and had been living in Paris.

Selma wept at the news; she wept often and as easily as trees shed leaves, even since her mother's death – or perhaps that was when Kate became old enough to notice it. It was a purely physical reaction, as involuntary as sneezing, Anne explained, and Kate could understand this: she also found that crying did her good – they said of her that she had settled too near the water. When she was little, she used to go about singing, at the top of her voice, ballads of her own invention to her out-of-tune versions of traditional songs, tears streaming out of her big grey eyes down her fat cheeks. Asked why she was crying, she used to explain, 'It's such a sad story.'

Selma went off to Wiesbaden to meet her stepmother. Apart from her one brief stay in hospital, she had never been separated from her daughters overnight. Kate got a couple of pimples on her left buttock, and thought that this was not something she could mention to anyone else. By the time Selma got back, after five days, they had grown into boils. Selma took her to their family doctor in Bielefeld, who lanced them. They returned to Brackwede by taxi, Kate lying on her stomach across Selma's knees. They were both of them crying. Selma said, 'I promise you, Putzi, never to leave you again.' Putzi was the commonest of the many terms of endearment she had for the baby of the family.

The name of Opa's new wife was Emma; it had also been their Oma's name but Selma could not bring herself to call the stranger mother.

The girls were told to call her Tante Emma.

She was tall, half a head taller than their Opa, a woman of authority. As she bent down to greet Kate she caught both her hands so that the child would not touch her; she could not kiss or be kissed because her mouth, her whole face was artificial with make-up. She smelled of pot-pourri, as if Opa had taken her out of storage; her every movement chimed with jewellery. She held herself as if balancing her head, as if balancing her crown of hair which shone blue like raven's feathers.

Her moving in transformed their Opa's home into a cross between a museum – where nothing may be touched – and something out of the Arabian Nights' Tales, where every surface was covered with something to look at, all made to seem other-worldly by tinted light. Her carpets and rugs were so luxurious that the doors needed re-hanging, her gilt-framed mirrors so tall that their legs needed to be sawn off. And oh, her chandeliers!

Her cooking was as exotic; it also found favour with the greedy Kate. In the days when their Oma had been alive, when the girls had come to the house she had fed them on cake, and Kate had not stopped eating until she felt too full to move. No one thought of curbing her appetite because she enjoyed her food so. While he had been without a wife, Opa had taken his family every Sunday afternoon into town, in his limousine, to the best café. There, an assortment of cakes was brought to their table on a three-tiered silver cake stand: you were allowed to choose again once your plate was empty. It conditioned Kate for the rest of her life to eat fast. While there was a cake left which she liked she went on eating, even when she was full; her vomiting afterwards became part of the tradition.

Tante Emma was not one to cater separately for children. At her table Kate discovered that there were adult foods which suited her taste: pickled gherkins, for instance, and herring roe (it may have been caviar). All Tante Emma's dinners were ceremonial feasts, reminiscent of the Passover ritual because of the late hour and because another language was spoken, but chiefly because so many people were gathered around the table.

Roger and Marguerite seemed more like cousins to the girls than uncle and aunt. Roger enthralled them with conjuring tricks, Marguerite, older, with her semi-adult and Parisian ways. They were the heralds of other relations, incomprehensible even when speaking German – for instance the woman who stitched up the pockets of her daughter's clothes so that she would not make use of them and thus spoil their shape. There was also an influx of strangers who were their Opa's relations and had all the time lived no further away than Hamelin – making Kate understand, though she was unwilling to do so, that most of her Opa's existence lay beyond her knowledge and for most of the time she – and what was worse, Anne – mattered not much to him.

Once, he took them to visit his relations in Hamelin. One of them was a blind woman, probably not as aged as she seemed to Kate, who sat on the couch beside her holding hands, neither of them wanting to let go. It was a phenomenon long spoken of in the family, how the blind woman's quiet ways had subdued the usually ebullient Kate.

'What made you so patient with her?' Anne asked. Kate did not know. Perhaps that she *was* blind, and therefore could not value Kate's company for the sake of Kate's appearance and must have had a better reason for wanting to hold her hand.

That was the year in which, for Hanukkah, the girls got ice-skates, all three of them because that was what Lise wished for. Kate learned to use them because she could not bear to be excluded from anything Lise did, but she hated it, and Anne never even tried. They got Norwegian jumpers – Anne's red, Lise's green, Kate's blue – these being considered their colours – of the same pattern with matching hats and mittens. They got a film projector, and two films of Charlie Chaplin and two of Mickey Mouse. Their father promised, 'When you're tired of them I'll buy you some more.' But he did not, because within a few weeks Hitler had come to power.

After those Christmas holidays, the older children came to school with packets of small stickers, with election slogans that meant nothing to Kate. She agreed to go about the village putting up red ones because that was Anne's colour. When Anne heard of it she laughed at her: Kate had chosen to support the communists. A good thing that she had not preferred the Nazi colour!

As if their Opa's second marriage had been no more than a theatrical performance, one day Tante Emma and all she had brought with her disappeared again out of their lives for ever.

Their Opa also went to France, but he came back. He had left behind him debts which he meant to settle by means of selling what remained of his assets. Instead of giving him the chance to do so, the Nazis imprisoned him as a defaulter. It must have been meant as a warning to the Jewish community: if they could do this to its president, then they could do anything.

He must have known that he was about to be arrested, or perhaps he was summoned to the police station and knew what to expect. He came to his daughter's house to speak with her and as he was leaving, pausing on the threshold of the verandah before going down the flight of steps, he said, 'Nothing was ever too good for them,' and burst into tears. He was speaking of his granddaughters, who were hanging about, baffled to be ignored, trying to catch his attention – Kate, below him, was at that moment reaching for his hand. They needed to prise her fingers away from it, because she did not want him to leave while he was crying.

That evening there were once again visitors in the house. They did not come until late, after even Anne had been sent upstairs to bed. But the girls were still awake and they could hear them. There was in the bedroom shared by Lise and Kate a chimney niche with a seat of mottled brown tiles, and a grille in the upright wall through which warm air came from the stove in the sitting-room. With your ear close to it you could hear what was being said below.

Most likely Anne had listened there before. In her night-dress, she came and of course Lise and Kate got out of bed again, Lise to listen with her and Kate to keep them company. The grille was not wide enough for three heads and she would anyway not have been able to make sense of what she heard. During a silence downstairs, Anne said that she had overheard their mother saying on the telephone that she was not allowed to bring him even a pillow: from this she knew that their Opa was now in prison. Kate believed Anne capable of making such deductions. 'What has he done wrong?' she asked, not yet doubting that the world was just.

Anne hushed her: the adults downstairs had begun to talk of emigrating. But she said, 'Give me a cardigan,' because she felt cold, and made do with putting one of Kate's about her shoulders because she was listening and did not want to miss one word.

The Nazis did no more than imprison the old man: it sufficed to destroy him. They did not want him to die in their custody – his philanthropy had not been confined to Jews – and so they returned him to his family.

Selma put him in Anne's room, in Anne's bed. The leaders of the community came and went, but only the doctor was allowed to see him. The house was kept quiet; even the loud Kate did not make much noise, so conscious was she of his frail presence. Selma, until now so cosseted, would not let anyone else do what could still be done for him. She appeared to be a milk and water woman, but she managed to keep him alive for three more days.

When he felt himself to be dying, he had his granddaughters called to him, one at a time. Naturally, Anne went in first. She came out with her chin held high, her face glowing with the blessing which had been bestowed upon her. Lise needed to be urged to take her turn – she feared not being equal to the occasion, which made her tremble from head to foot in anticipation, and also afterwards. Kate, as always, even at that moment resented being the one who came last. Waiting, she remembered how the patriarch Isaac had exhausted the blessing he had to give before Esau could take his turn.

Her Opa's head was lying low; it looked smaller than his importance in her life had led her to expect. His lips moved but made no sound. Behind her, her mother said, 'He wants to kiss you.' How? Where? She had never known her grandfather so passive. Unused to doing anything for the first time without having at least Lise's example to follow, she cheated: bent down but only pretended to put her cheek against his lips. He seemed to her to be too ill to notice or, noticing, care. He looked past her at her mother and her mother, who could not have seen the cheating from where she stood, lifted his hand up and laid it on Kate's head.

'*Baruch* . . .' he whispered, and ceased. Selma had more strength of body and mind than Kate knew when she was a child: she laid her hand over her father's and let her go on standing there for long enough to allow her to believe that she, too, had been blessed.

But Kate believed that the blessing was worthless because she had not deserved it.

Selma told Anne to take her sisters for a walk. She did not want them to watch the body being carried out of the house.

The three girls went round the houses and gardens to where, between these and the forest, there was a coppice which Lise and Kate thought of as theirs because they had always been allowed to play in it unsupervised, even in the days of the Düsseldorf child murders. They had made a den there which they had long wanted to show to Anne. 'It wouldn't be right for me to look at it now,' she ruled. 'Now we mustn't enjoy ourselves.'

But for Kate it was enjoyable just to have her company.

They remained on the edge of the coppice, standing with their backs to the trees and looking towards the houses; only the roofs could be seen and Kate did not know which one was theirs. But she knew what Lise was waiting for: to see the angel of death descending, or to see him ascending with their Opa's soul.

Anne said, 'The ambulance has come, I can see them carrying Opa out on a stretcher.'

'I can't see anything,' Kate complained, and Anne told her that that was because she was too little. Such was Kate's faith in her that not until thirty years later – when she stood, again, alone, where they had stood on that day – did she realize that Anne, too, had not been able to see anything.

Because Anne did not allow her feelings to show, Kate believed that she was not grieving and so did not grieve, convinced that it was better for their Opa's soul to have discarded his body. That she could not imagine his survival did not make her doubt it: it was what those around her believed, or at least did not disbelieve with sufficient conviction to say so.

Selma once more put on mourning; she continued to wear black until made to exchange it for concentration camp uniform. She used to say that she was wearing mourning for the Jews of Germany.

At the time of Opa's arrest his house was sealed up; after his death its contents were confiscated. The removal van was too big to be driven up to the door, so everything had to be carried down the garden path and through the gate. Selma and her daughters stood by, not allowed to touch anything, though Selma was given without argument the few things – such as a work-box and a vase – which she claimed were her own. Kate marvelled at her – since Jews were such criminals – for not claiming more than her due.

The house next door to them had been standing empty. It was now rented by a high-ranking Nazi who demanded that alterations be made to the verandah. For the sake of symmetry – this was the middle house in the row – the owners decided to make the same alterations to both sides and suggested to the Loewenthals, to spare them having the builders in, that they should move to the house in which Opa had lived. This they did. They had not previously had a garage, which became both storage space and a playroom for Lise and Kate.

Ever since coming to Brackwede, they had played with the son of their other neighbours, called Klaus, then a baby. He now had a brother; they had been fascinated by the mother's pregnancy. Now, to get to the Wehmeyers, they took to walking along the continuous brick wall at the back of the courtyards. It was a man-high drop on their side (they needed a chair to climb on to it) though much less on the other. They thought nothing of still doing so after the new people had moved in.

One day when they were walking along the wall, they saw the new people through the window, sitting eating. They stopped to wave; to do this they first sat down. Before they had got up again to walk on, a young man – the son of the house – came out with a glass in his hand. He threw water at them. Never before in their lives – such had been their status in society – had they encountered hostility from a stranger.

A day or two later, they were playing in the garden when the young man next door called to them over the box hedge. 'See my dog?' It was a German shepherd. 'If you Jews don't behave yourselves, I shall set him on you – he is a trained killer.'

Fear had entered their everyday.

Going to the Bible class was just about the only thing Kate did without Lise – she did not even go to the lavatory without her when she had the choice. Only once, Lise came with her to the Bible class, perhaps at the suggestion of their mother, who wished to know what went on there. Even on that occasion Kate did not want her to come: that she went there by herself was part of the allure. If Lise were to like it, would she not always want to come? And whatever Lise did not like instantly lost for Kate half its attraction.

On the way there, Kate told her, 'This is my thing, I discovered it. I'm a member of the class and you're going to be only a visitor. Nobody will want you to say anything.' It could be embarrassing, on occasion, what Lise came out with: she sometimes had peculiar ideas and was so shy, so mortified by attention, that she could not express, explain or defend them, and thus in Kate's opinion made a fool of herself.

Kate stopped walking and said, 'I won't take you', but she could not have prevented her from going, 'unless you promise that you won't spoil it for me.' Lise would not knowingly have spoiled anything for her. Perhaps it was a revelation to Lise that Kate said this. Perhaps Kate believed that Jesus would prefer the meek and mild Lise and that was why she was reluctant to let her come.

The Bible class also attracted Kate because attending it made her feel guilty and that was something she relished, mistaking it for evidence of having been brave. She did not accept that as a Jew she was one of the Christ-killers: she knew that, on the contrary, had she been there she would have done everything possible to defend him, and so she did not feel guilty on that account. What she felt guilty about was wanting to be one of the little children who came to Jesus. She also felt guilty because the Bible class children did something her mother would have disapproved of Kate doing had she known – that not even Lise knew of it augmented the guilt.

They visited the old and the sick in their homes and sang hymns to them, and no one ever told her not to join in because she sang out of tune or did not sound mellow. The louder she sang the more the Protestant sisters smiled at her. 'You like to praise Jesus, don't you,' was the only comment they made.

One day that spring, when having been to an outlying farmstead had made them late, Kate, on her way home, near the top of the hill, was met by her mother, who stopped when she saw her and shouted, 'Where have you been? Don't you know that you are a Jew!'

It was not only the shouting in the street by her mother who, when they had come to Brackwede, had bought a gong with which to summon her daughters in from play so as not to have to raise her voice in public (she did not ever raise it, even at home). It was also the asking of a question to which she knew the answer; it was the reproach for doing something which had her implied permission. Above all it was the calling out, there in the street for all to hear, that execration, which had for Kate, on the mental plane, the effect of a grenade.

Four

That summer, a neighbour's cat had a litter of kittens. Kate happened to see them over the hedge one day when their basket had been put out in the garden. She went back again and again to look for them, and when they were there look at them – hoping with half her mind that she would not be seen and told to go away, and with the other half that someone would see her and invite her in. And that was what happened.

The mother cat was a tabby; four of the kittens were like her but one was black. She had not known until then that they were born with blue eyes. She thought the black one sweetest because it was the outsider.

'May I come back and stroke them again?' she asked when she thought that the woman standing over her might be getting impatient, and when the answer was slow in coming added, 'Just once – sometime when it suits you?' Seven months of the Hitler regime had taught her caution in her dealings with Aryans.

'Would you like to have one when they're old enough to leave their mother?' the woman asked her.

Kate was convinced that the reason why she was offered a kitten was that the owner did not want a Jew coming into her garden.

She hesitated to mention it at home, believing that a kitten would be too expensive, assessing its price by its value in her own eyes. She waited for an opportunity to ask the neighbour how much it would cost. She tried, and failed, to relate it to her Jewishness when she was told that she could have it for nothing.

Her father had closed his office; he had given up being an architect and gone into business selling pigs' feed. It was mixed to his own recipe in big vats in the cellar and put into strong brown paper bags printed with the name he called it and a picture of sundry contented, thriving pigs: his own design. The dust from the handling settled all over the cellar; the pungent smell permeated the whole house. Their Nazi neighbour had complained to the landlord; they had been given notice.

They were anyway no longer able to afford the rent. When Kate asked if she could have a kitten, her mother said, 'You know that we're going to move. We won't be able to have a cat where we're going.' As yet, they had nowhere to go, but Selma knew what she was looking for.

'Perhaps we'll at least have a tiny garden?' Kate wheedled.

When she had been little enough to be given a box of bricks for Hanukkah, she had built a tower with them and told Anne, 'There, that is my present to you!' When Anne had asked her, did she really mean to give her new bricks away? she had answered, 'The sight is your present.' The term Hanukkah-sight became part of the family language.

Selma agreed to let Kate have a kitten as a sort of prolonged Hanukkah-sight, on the understanding that she would give it up without argument when they moved. When the neighbour asked her which one she wanted, she could not make up her mind. She liked the black one best – but since there were more tabbies, were they not better? She remained undecided; she must have hoped to be left without choice but when she was told that there were only two not yet spoken for, one of them the black, she suddenly felt so fiercely protective towards it that she insisted on taking it away at once although the owner told her that it was not yet really old enough.

There was among the poems in Kate's school-book – she had all of them by heart – one about a boy who is told by his parents to drown the kitten he has; he obeys but is instantly sorry enough to jump in after it – and regains consciousness lying in bed, with the kitten on the window-sill. Reciting the poem to herself or even thinking of it, Kate found her eyes overflowing; when the time came, she planned, she would use it to make her mother change her mind.

If it had been up to him, Paul would have fathered more children, if only because he would have liked to have had a son. But after Kate's birth Selma had had enough. It was perhaps because no other baby came along that Selma so overwhelmed Kate with mothering; perhaps because Kate resented it so, Selma needed to find an excuse for it, and this was what made her think of her youngest as delicate – which she wasn't.

She was always pale. For no more than that reason, Selma repeatedly took her to the family doctor, who, after dutifully examining her, used to say, 'She's just thick-skinned.' Kate learned to expect this, and understood that it was to be taken literally. Nevertheless, it mortified her: she would have preferred her body to be a more faithful incarnation of her character as she saw it.

In time she learned to take advantage of her mother's anxiety, and got out of things which she did not want to do – going for walks in the winter cold, for instance – by pretending to have a stomach ache or, preferable because she liked to eat, a headache. Who could prove her a liar? But either she was too sanguine or Selma could read the signals better than Kate gave her credit for. Towards the end of that summer, Kate found herself disbelieved on one occasion when she was speaking the truth.

She had a terrible pain behind her forehead.

School had just started again and Selma may have thought that Kate for some reason did not want to attend; it was in keeping with Selma's ways that, though disbelieving her, she allowed her to stay at home. She even suggested that she should lie down in the parental bedroom, in her mother's bed – so much softer than her own and comprehensively comforting – so as to have the sun shining in on her. The bright light aggravated Kate's headache.

On the third day, in mid-morning, she was roused by her mother asking, 'What's wrong with you, what's hurting?' If she had been pretending, Kate would have invented another pain, but the one she had felt to her like reason enough for staying where she was. 'Maybe what you need is a little fresh air,' her mother said, and suggested that she should go down the hill to the grocer's. Though it did not require the crossing of the main road, this was the first time in her life that she was given such an adult errand.

She got herself up, and put on the clothes which her mother handed to her, sitting down to the job as much as possible. Normally,

she argued over what to wear. When Selma had sent picture postcards from Wiesbaden, Kate's had been of a cat in a pink frock in
front of a mirror, a half empty wardrobe, and discarded choices all
over the floor; underneath it said, 'Pink suits me excellently.' It had
become one of the family sayings, used against Kate when she was
being vain. But Selma and even Anne took pleasure in her appearance and Selma often said so. (Lise was forbidden by Kate to comment on it.) Anne once said to Kate, 'You'd look all right if you were
wearing a sack.'

That day her frock was a dirndl of poplin, light blue with a pattern
of hearts in dark-blue and white, with heart-shaped white buttons. It
was special because she had chosen the material herself, in company
not with her mother but her father, who had got it and a length of
suiting from a shopkeeper owing him money. The Jews had begun to
barter, though mostly still only among themselves.

It felt strange to Kate to be going about the village while all the
other children were in school; it made her feel self-consciously important. This was the last time she was to believe herself singled out
in a benevolent way; she thought everybody was looking at her and
thinking, that child is ill and ought to be in bed. It cheered her up to
imagine people believing that she had a bad mother, because it
allowed her to contradict them in her mind and thus reassure herself.

To get her to take this walk, Selma had told her to buy a tin of Van
Houten's drinking chocolate, which tasted so much nicer than the
cocoa they had been using lately; she had been asking for it ever since
the beginning of her headache. There were other things on the
shopping-list which she had been given; when she saw them piling up
on the counter, she thought that she would not have the strength to
carry them. She asked for them to be sent. Making the decision to say
this and saying it, meant behaving as if she were Anne. It made her
uneasy: she would not have wished Anne or even Lise to have such a
headache.

With only the tin of drinking chocolate to carry in a string bag
hanging from her wrist, she set off back up the hill. By the time she
had got half-way her legs had grown so weak and unwilling that she
used what little strength she had in her arms to help them along,
holding hand over hand on to the railings of other people's gardens,

hoping not to be seen or, if seen, not to be recognized as a Jew. Just as she was about to be overcome by the temptation to sit down on the pavement like a tramp, she saw her mother coming towards her, in search of her, because the errand was taking her so long.

Big as she was – ten years old – she was carried home by her mother.

When the family had moved to Brackwede, they had kept as their doctor Dr Griesbach in Bielefeld. Until the beginning of that year, Selma would not have hesitated for so many days before asking him to come. Even now she did not do that, because of the cost. Instead, after lunch, she took Kate to him, by tram.

For the past two winters, they had made that journey once a week for Kate to have her suppurating tonsils squeezed. It had become a tradition that, afterwards, they went to the shops to buy her some small present as a recompense for what she had had to put up with. She usually chose a book and was still at the stage of wanting fabulous stories.

That day, on the way, she asked if this time, too, they would afterwards go to buy a present: her headache was certainly something for which she deserved compensation. Her mother answered, 'If it will make you feel better.' Kate thought that feeling better was now for ever beyond her.

Dr Griesbach took one look at her and told Selma, 'You ought not to have brought her out.' He took Kate's temperature and pronounced it to be over forty. 'Go home by taxi, you must,' he told Selma, and tried to give her the money but she would not accept it. He summoned a taxi to his door and paid for the journey in advance. Kate had paratyphoid.

The source of the infection may have been the kitten: when they came to move out, evidence of its diarrhoea was found all over the cellar, where it had spent the nights. Lise and Kate had known all along that its motions were liquid and light yellow. One day it shat in the kitchen after Marie had just washed the floor; she refused to deal with it. Because it never took much to make Kate vomit – they had just eaten, and their mother had gone upstairs for her afternoon nap – Lise volunteered to clean up, while Kate took the kitten to sit with it under the pear tree. She made Lise promise not to tell their mother.

It was a notifiable disease. The district medical officer came, with the district health inspector, to arrange Kate's hospitalization. Selma refused even to consider it. 'Your other daughters will catch the infection,' they warned her. She said that she would make certain that they did not. 'You will catch it.' Not while her child needed her. 'If you separate her from me she will die,' Kate overheard her saying.

Either moved by this Jewess, or unconcerned about Jews, they gave in to her.

The wallpaper was brick red, patterned with shapes of leaves in darker tones and with touches of gold. The woodwork and the ceiling were dove grey. Kate's bed stood in a corner diagonally opposite the door, a window to the left of her head and another to the right of her feet. The room looked very empty with Lise's bed gone.

Her feather pillow was large and square, its red ticking covered with a starched white slip. There was a loose damask cover, also white and starched, on her feather duvet; its own cover was of glazed cotton with a bold bright floral pattern on a blue background. Her sisters had covers like it, each in her own colour.

Anne bit her nails to the quick until she was in her mid-teens; Lise had a callosity on her thumb from sucking it in the privacy of her bed, even after exchanging home for England. Kate's vice was both more secret and more terrible: she masturbated. If the others did so, nobody knew about it. Kate was discovered, still in Roland Street, lying on her stomach with crossed thighs and rocking. They then put on her nightly a leather gadget designed to keep her legs parallel. It happened when she was old enough to undo the buckles but still so young that this came as a surprise.

She had an even greater passion for telling herself stories, but for more than a fortnight she did not even do that. She lay still with her eyes closed, night and day, falling asleep as if she were dying and surprised to wake up again. All that time, the headache remained her incubus. She could not be bothered to eat or drink, or to speak, or even to wish herself better. If this was what being alive was like, she thought, she would rather be dead. When she began to get better she said something like this to her mother, who said, 'Put a stop to it, Putzi.' Out of a mixture of boredom and devilment, Kate had begun to pick through the wallpaper into the plaster, where it was hidden by her bedding; now she revealed the hole, the size of her fingertip, saying, 'This is the stop.' Selma thought it enough of a joke to feel reassured that Kate would live.

Sometimes, without crossing the threshold, Anne, more often Lise, looked past Selma as she went in or out. They had been doing so for two weeks before Kate became aware of it. She felt estranged enough from them not to be curious about what they had meanwhile been doing, and still weak enough not to mind that they were not yet allowed to come in. For once, she was not impatient to be getting on with her life. It was as if she had known, subliminally, that the world to which she was recovering was no longer the same.

Anne and Lise were not allowed to go to school. Selma was not allowed to leave the house. Paul was not allowed to go near Kate. No restriction had been placed on the contact between Selma and Paul; it did not make sense but the family obeyed the rules.

There came the day when Kate asked for her father. 'I just want to look at him,' she pleaded, not wanting to admit that she had forgotten what he looked like.

She was told that he was out; he was always either out or she was asleep. Selma did not tell her that out of the house meant away from home, because she could not have talked about it without weeping, and egocentric Kate might have misinterpreted her tears. He was travelling around, as far as Cologne in one direction and as far as Hanover in the other, visiting old comrades and anyone else he could think of who might provide him with work. It was doing no good and costing money that was needed to keep the household going.

One morning, when Kate was at the stage of being able to sit up but tiring quickly, her mother asked her if there were anything she wanted: Marie would soon be going down to the shops. 'A peach,' Kate said. 'A notebook and –' Delighted that her interests were reviving, Selma suggested that she should make a list.

Once Kate began to think about what she could do now that she was beginning to feel better, she realized that there were lots of things she wanted. For instance, balls of wool, as many different colours as possible, for making doll's clothes on the knitting-frame which she had got for her birthday and hardly had time to enjoy.

Taking the list, and seeing the length of it, her mother said, 'I haven't the money to get you all of this.'

Then why had she told her to write down what she wanted? All she had asked for were only little things. She was bewildered by her mother suddenly counting the cost of pleasing her – when she had been so ill. Knowing that she was being unreasonable, she said, 'If I were dead I wouldn't be costing you money, maybe you're sorry that I didn't die!' She needed to hear her mother contradict her. But she was also ashamed of herself and hid her head under her duvet.

With her usual infinite patience, Selma coaxed her out, and began to explain more than Kate was able or willing to understand. At first she would not even listen. What got through to her was her mother saying, 'We can no longer afford to buy clothes for ourselves, your dolls will have to manage without new clothes.'

But then, Kate argued, the knitting-frame had been a waste of money! She wasn't thinking of herself, saying this, but of her dolls. Perhaps her brain was still too addled with illness for her to understand just then that unlike herself, her dolls did not grow out of their things.

She should have some wool, Selma said; she should have all possible combinations of colours by getting three variegated balls. And together they went through the shopping-list, making the necessary compromises.

Her father, at last allowed to come to her bedside, brought her a doll made of dark red celluloid. She was not sure whether or not to believe what he told her, that it was unique (perhaps a free sample?), but she was never to come across another like it. She thought it fortunate that she had wool for her knitting-frame, because it arrived naked. Any present from her father was special just because it came from him, but she could not like the red doll: by word association, it made her think of Red Indians, which reminded her of what happened to minorities.

50

Her father spoke of bringing her another present. He said that he had seen, in a toy-shop window, a big furry cat which could walk and mew – he had wondered if she would like to have it. She thought that, within the family, no one except him would have needed to ask her that question. 'Oh, yes!' she exclaimed with more fervour than she had yet managed since she had been ill. He promised to get it for her the very next day. Selma, who had a better idea than he what toys cost – and was less optimistic – may have nudged him, because he added, 'If it hasn't been sold.'

Throughout the following afternoon, and all evening, Kate waited not so much for her father as for his present. She objected to having the light switched off, and even afterwards tried not to go to sleep before it came. Selma had placed a chair level with her pillow for the cat to be put on, and left the curtains open a little for the moonlight to shine through, so that Kate would be able to see it once it was there. Again and again, in the course of that night, she struggled out of sleep. And still the chair was empty – or so it looked to her.

A big white cat, her father had promised, much bigger than the kitten, which had gone and she avoided thinking about. No one except Paul would so thoughtlessly have reminded her of it. As his daughters grew older his tactlessness became proverbial with them. But now Kate consoled herself with the thought that a toy cat was better because she would be able to take it into her bed and cuddle it all night long, and to make up for it not being alive it would never, never leave her. It did not come.

As it began to grow light, Kate could see that the chair was not as empty as she had believed. On it was a dog, about as big as her hand, its fur of a mottled light brown. A terrier, it looked not unlike the dog she had once tried to adopt. But it was not what she wanted. It was not what she had been led to expect and she did not want it.

It was in a squatting position, it squeaked when its flanks were pressed and its head could be moved by means of turning its tail. Her mother demonstrated this to her, striving to reconcile her to it before her father got up and came to ask her how she liked his present. The cat had cost too much. 'He could ill afford to buy even this,' her mother told her. 'He got it to please you.'

Later that day, to help make the dog acceptable to Kate, she suggested naming it. Most likely it was she who suggested *Lümmel*, meaning hooligan – a love-hate name – and then suggested that it be toned down to Lümmi. She helped Kate to make a song about it, Kate supplying the words and her mother the tune.

All the cats had been sold, her father told her; that dog was the nearest thing to what he had promised her left in the shop. He could say this looking straight into her eyes. Kate blamed her mother for having told her the truth, without which she would not have known that he was lying. As far as she knew he had never before chosen a present – as distinct from paying for it – for any of his daughters. She tried to be satisfied with his having chosen it for her.

But like the goatskin in front of her bed, it served as a constant reminder that her parents could not be entirely relied upon.

Five

Theesener Street marked the boundary of the town; to the right of it lay open fields. Where Kügler Street ran into it from the left it stopped being a made-up road and continued as a track across waste ground on which there was a disused brick factory. The last dwelling-house was an L-shaped tenement with, built into the corner of it, a grocer's shop. On the other corner stood a six-family house – address 16 Kügler Street. When Selma first went there both the ground-floor flats were vacant.

It was a ground-floor flat she was looking for because she suffered badly from varicose veins. She brought her family to help her choose or rather, to approve of the choice which she had already more or less made. The flat on the right had not one but two rooms facing the open fields, and one room which faced the garden, and its balcony faced the garden instead of the road. (Most of the garden was taken up by a patch of grass not worthy of being called a lawn, on which there were posts for the clothes-lines; there was also a metal frame rather like goal-posts, for beating carpets. The outer flat had a small private garden; the tenants of this one had to make do with only a flower-bed in the communal one.)

There was a vestibule, spacious but of little use because its only light was from the amber and blue panes in the front door. The bathroom was narrow and included the lavatory. The kitchen was large, with a big window and a glass door leading on to the balcony: it was pleasant enough to make a living-room. The other flat had four rooms; this one had three, one of which Paul would need to use as his office.

'And where am I supposed to sleep?' Anne asked. To Lise and Kate, the proposed move was an adventure, but Anne was old enough to understand what it meant for the family.

'Supposing we take the other flat, will that make you happy?' Selma asked her.

Anne was selfish but she was also a realist: having a room of her own would make no difference to everything else that was going wrong with their lives. She must have relished having it in her power to make their mother, at that moment, glad about something.

To have remained in Brackwede beyond the end of September because of Kate's illness would have meant paying another month's rent. It was cheaper to hire an ambulance to transfer her to Kügler Street.

The three girls had identical white metal bedsteads; Selma sent one ahead to be set up in the empty flat against Kate's arrival. She travelled with her, leaving the supervision of the removal to Paul and Marie, and telling Lise that she should stand in for her. Lise took the responsibility so much to heart that she came to believe that she alone – eleven years old – had been left in charge.

Anne, on that day, went to school as usual, and came to the flat only when it was already approximately their home.

The bed for Kate had been placed in a corner of what was to be her parents' bedroom. The wallpaper was leaf-green. This pleased Selma, who believed that green was a calming colour; she put up curtains of a darker shade. Here, after a day or two, Kate had her first visitor, Tante Hete, only distantly related – the family had no close relations at all in Bielefeld.

Tante Hete argued with Selma that, on the contrary, red was the colour which calmed. It agitated the feelings and made one compensate, because all nature constantly strove for balance. She also said that Kate's having been so ill was really a blessing: though God had allowed them to come down in the world, he had with Kate's recovery provided them with something for which to praise him.

Tante Hete and Onkel Max Sieger were sent to Theresienstadt: he died there; she was sent on to Auschwitz and did not survive.

The present which she brought Kate was the book *Pinocchio*. Kate loved the story. She constantly demanded that her mother should leave her work and sit down to listen. Later Selma used to say that it was this book which had restored Kate's interest in life.

Once Kate was allowed out of bed, she sat in her father's leather armchair which now stood by the kitchen window, and Lise brought the neighbourhood children to stand, one by one, on the cellar-step railings while she mouthed their names, already familiar to Kate from what she had told her about them. Few could resist the chance to take a look at the pale, frail girl who had arrived by ambulance and remained imprisoned like a fairytale princess. No Jew had ever lived in this working-class district; the term meant nothing there yet. The Third Reich was not yet a year old.

The railings were fixed to the side of the balcony, and by means of them you could climb up on to it. Lise and Kate were at first still young enough for this to be their favourite way of entering the flat – through the bathroom window if the door to the kitchen was locked. There was a space under the balcony which became their den, concrete replacing the forest. Here their friends came to crouch, to hear Lise sing and Kate tell stories.

The first time Kate was allowed out, one sunny Sunday afternoon in mid-October, and walked, arms linked, between her parents, most of the neighbourhood children were there to watch: Lise had alerted them. One little girl stepped forward and presented Kate with a bunch of late wild flowers. Overcome by the occasion, she did it with a curtsy which was greeted by the onlookers with applause – or were they applauding Kate?

She was furious with Lise, knowing that she would not be able to live up to such a reception.

Lise, exploring their new surroundings on behalf of them both, had discovered the way back to Roland Street. Kate must have been homesick for the past even then: the first time she was allowed to go out with Lise, she insisted on going there, straight away. She was not interested in going anywhere else. Lise, as always, gave in to her. To her it must not have seemed very far.

Their intention had been to go first to the house where they had been born, and from there, by the route by which they used to be taken, to their beloved park. Close to their old house was an open space, Siegfried Square, large enough for a market to be held there once a week. It was triangular in shape, and in the middle of its base were the police headquarters, with a high and wide flight of shallow steps leading up to the doors. This also was where, when they were little, they used to play. On the occasion of that first pilgrimage, they rested there. As Kate was exhausted she was incapable of going further and Lise carried her pick-a-back all the way home.

To give Anne privacy, Selma divided the girls' room with a curtain made of transparent material – beige with a pattern of ears of corn and flowers found in a cornfield – hung from a rail fixed well below the ceiling. Anne did not want her part to serve as a corridor to the others and so was given the end by the window. Lise and Kate wanted her to have it, not only so as to be able to go freely in and out of their part, but because the window part was better and therefore Anne's due. 'Well, you have the stove,' she pointed out. She always managed to make it look as if she were the one who was doing the others a favour.

The curtain was hers, and was under her jurisdiction. She decreed when it was to be open and when it was to be closed. It was almost always closed when she was in her part, which the others were not allowed to enter except with her permission, so rarely granted that they learned to wait until she invited them in – when, for instance, she wanted to play chess with Kate. They were supposed never to touch the curtain without her permission, but in time it came to be understood that they could open it when she was not at home.

Lise and Kate shared their mother's wardrobe, Anne had a small one of her own. All three had bedside cabinets; she also had a table, which stood under the window, and of course a chair to go with it. Her wash-stand had its own mirror. Much of the furniture they had had in Brackwede had been sold at the time of the move for much less than its real value, making more Germans grateful to Hitler. For the girls' bedroom it had been replaced with cheaper things, all painted white.

Perhaps Anne kept the curtain closed because she did not want anyone to see her practising her habit of touching corners. It became a compulsion: she did it in a fixed sequence with both hands, raising her right one to touch also the lock of hair on her forehead, every time before she left her room. It was something not to be mentioned.

Most of the carpets had also been sold, and Lise and Kate had none. Kate had her goatskin; Anne had the red and beige carpet which, in Brackwede, had been in the maid's room. (For a while, in Kügler Street, they still had Marie, but now she was employed by the hour.) At some time in the course of the next two years, Anne upset her bottle of ink as she lay on the floor doing her homework. She did not want an ink-stained carpet; she told Lise and Kate that they could have it. It went against the order of the universe as Kate saw it, that they should have a carpet while Anne had none – by then there was no question of finding the money to replace it. Kate solved the problem by giving Anne her goatskin to cover the stain.

Kate used to ask Lise, 'If I were not your sister, would you still be my friend?' to which Lise answered, 'Of course I would, you are my best friend, you are the only real friend I have.' These words had long ago been chosen for her by Kate, who needed to hear them.

Kate was not much good at making friends. She believed that any child willing to make friends with the likes of her was not really worth being friends with. Whenever she did make friends, she did not share them with Lise. Having from birth preferred Lise's company to her own, she was convinced that everybody must do so, and she did not want to be friends with people who preferred Lise.

Much of the time Lise's friends were the only ones Kate had. Lise shared her friends with her as she shared everything. Lise was willing – and able – to make friends with any child, believing that those no one else wanted were the ones who needed her most. Lise was just then growing a lot and losing weight. Squeezed between the stronger personalities of her sisters, she sought to define herself through idiosyncracies. She believed that God had singled her out for a mission though she did not yet know what it was.

Their Opa would have been appalled to see his younger grand-daughters playing in those streets. Why did Selma allow it? Perhaps she felt their lives hurtling beyond her control, or she did not want to add to the restrictions beginning to be imposed on them by the state. Or she may have believed that coming from what she thought of as a good family, a good home, and going to a good school, armoured them against street influences. The worst mischief they ever got up to was joining the bell-chasers on cold dark nights – kids who rang doorbells and then ran away. Also, they joined in cheering on the boys who threw stones to smash the street lamps.

But most of their playing-time was taken up with skipping-ropes and ball games, all of which Lise was good at, and she was generous enough to allow others to win. She would not have joined in without Kate, who was welcomed for her sake, and also for her looks. But taking them under the balcony was the nearest they came to bringing their street friends home – they knew that their mother would not have approved of them. They did not keep themselves or their clothing clean and neat – until they joined the Hitler Youth and became self-respecting by despising all non-Nazis.

By the spring, there began to be children who would not play with Lise and Kate because they were Jews, or who were summoned away from playing with them by their parents or older siblings. But not for another year or so did some start throwing stones at them. Then they were no longer allowed to enter the tenement courtyard. The last time they did so, a woman on her balcony emptied a bucket of water over them. There were then also adults who, in passing, swore at them.

By then they were too old anyway to play in the street.

Anne and Lise attended the Sarepta girls' high school in Bethel, which lay in the hills between Bielefeld and Brackwede. Bethel was a devoutly Christian community, dedicated to the care of the physically and the mentally ill from all over Germany. The school had no connection with these institutions. Paul and Selma had chosen it for their daughters because it was the nearest girls' high school to Brackwede; they continued to send them there after the move to Kügler Street – which made it the furthest away – because its headmaster was one of Paul's comrades from the trenches. No other Jewish girls attended this school. Kate was to start there only after Easter; when she returned to school after her illness it was to the local elementary one.

Serving a working-class district, its children were rougher than village children; none went barefoot, but many had lice in their hair. Kate instantly took to her class teacher because, though fairly young, somehow he reminded her of her grandfather. Herr Lehmann, when the class became rowdy, took out his violin and played, and played, ignoring the pandemonium, and ignored by the children until their ringleaders were ready to quieten down again. Such self-control seemed to Kate a heroic virtue. One day she waited until everyone else had gone, and then, trembling with apprehension as if she were Lise, she said to him, 'I want you to know that at least one of us listens to your playing.' She said it not to curry favour but to comfort him. He answered that he played not for them but for himself. If it made him think about Kate he did not show it.

In Brackwede, Kate had been encouraged to make her writing small; now she was told to make it larger. She found it difficult to make it both large and even. In her calligraphy exercise book, she tore out the page, and the corresponding page at the back (as she had once watched Anne doing) again and again, in order to make a fresh start, until it showed that there were pages missing. Then she took a new exercise book, and did not shrink from copying into it, as nicely as possible, all the term's previous work. In time she came to do the same in all the subjects; she would rather spend her pennies on replacing her school exercise books than on buying sweets. She was a glutton for filling blank pages; the activity gave her a physical satisfaction.

The class had already begun to rehearse the Christmas play. To thaw the shy new girl out they cast her as an additional angel.

'I don't think it's right for her to take part,' her mother said as the family sat at table. 'They can't be aware that she's Jewish.' If this was so, Kate wanted nothing to be done about it. But what would happen when they discovered that she was a Jew – as they were bound to do sooner or later – *after* she had taken part? She was entitled to do that, Anne argued, as Jesus himself had been a Jew. Kate had not known or had forgotten this.

The angels were to sing carols. Kate did not know the words but did not say so, fearing that it would make the other children laugh at her (her idea of torture); and that the teacher in charge of rehearsals (a woman and the antithesis of Herr Lehmann) would deprive her of taking part. With all her capacity for wanting she wanted to be an angel, for the sake of the gold braid on her shift and wings, but also because being excluded from anything always forced her to face that she was a lesser child. When it came to the performance in front of an audience of parents, she only pretended to sing for fear that the words would come out wrong. Selma, who watched, afterwards told her that it had not showed. Kate was not reassured: if it had done, Selma (and Lise) would not have told her so. Only Anne and their father never spared her the truth.

Before Kate began to attend the Sarepta school, Anne said to her, 'I depend on you not to disgrace me, as you did when you started school in Brackwede. If I have to hear about you from any of the teachers, it had better be something good. Don't expect me to help you if you get into trouble. I'm paying you a compliment when I say that you must manage on your own because it implies that I believe you can. And don't come to me in the playground, it would embarrass me before my friends. I've had to earn my position and I won't let you jeopardize it. It's bad enough for me that Lise is in the form below.'

Anne, then in the lower fourth, was top of her class. Lise was reacting to the growing discrimination against her by failing in her school work. Kate, as always, copied Anne – with such determination that she got even higher marks.

Lise did not believe that Kate would be able to manage on her own. She took her firmly by the hand and showed her to her classroom, though Kate told her not to, would rather have gone there by herself in the hope that her classmates would form their first opinion of her without knowing that she was Jewish, and that it would outlast their prejudices once they found out.

Every other girl knew at least somebody there; she knew no one. 'What school are you from?' they asked her, and turned away, never having heard of it. Girls from her neighbourhood, if they went on to a high school at all, did not go to one like the Sarepta.

There was one girl in particular she noticed, with short blond hair and spirited blue eyes – lovely to look at. Others had noticed her too, formed a ring around her; Kate had to move this way and that so as to see all of her. She could not get close enough to hear, in the hubbub, what she was saying. Judging by the faces of those who stood closer, it was worth hearing.

She was Ingrid Modersohn. Kate, with her catastrophic penchant for loving beyond her reach (as she loved Anne), decided to make this girl choose her as her best friend. It took her a year to achieve it.

What encouraged her from the first was that, alphabetically, their names came next to each other; she saw this as an omen. They were made to seat themselves alphabetically to begin with; later the dunces would sit at the front and the élite at the back. 'Please, God . . .' Kate prayed as the teacher read out the names. Her surname came between Ingrid's and Lore's, but Lore asked to be allowed to sit in her place, because she and Ingrid knew each other; they were already best friends.

Until they quarrelled, Ingrid needed no other.

Kate believed that Anne did not want to be seen in public in the company of her sisters because Lise looked Jewish. But she did not want to be seen in Kate's company either, except on special occasions of her (Anne's) choosing – and there were times when she chose to go out with Lise.

Lise and Kate, as a matter of course, went to and from school together. Walking so as to be able to spend their tram-fare on something else came about by accident and took hold gradually. They got no pocket-money. If Selma still managed to give them enough to eat, what they got from her did not include such luxuries as sweets and chocolates. There was a confectioner's at the stop from which they started their journey home. They had to take two trams, changing on the Jahnplatz which was the town centre. Waiting, they always studied the display and one day, when Kate felt either especially hungry (school finished at one o'clock) or especially greedy, it occurred to her that if they were to walk to the Jahnplatz, they would have some pennies to spend.

To walk the whole way took about an hour, and provided them with money enough to buy paperback books, and whatever else they wanted if they saved up for it.

There was bound to come a day when Selma would ask, 'Where did you get the money to buy that?' Until then, they had made her believe that they were being kept at school longer, or rather, Kate had told her so after making Lise promise that she would not contradict her.

'We didn't tell you because we didn't want Papa to know,' Kate argued. 'What difference does it make to him, how we spend the money that he gives us?'

With their mother's connivance, they could set out early enough to walk to school in the mornings as well. It did not make them quite as rich as they had hoped. It worked out cheaper to buy booklets of tickets and they were expected to do that, except when their father did not have that much cash. He told them not to come to him all three at once, and whenever it was Lise's turn, it took her days to summon the determination to ask him for money which she could have managed without. Her scruples threatened to betray the deceit they were practising in addition to losing them money.

'As long as he can still afford to buy cigarettes . . .' Kate argued with her. It was what their mother had said when she had found them out.

In fact Paul, neither self-centred nor unobservant, must have known what was going on. Selma may well have told him. He may well have continued to behave as expected of him by his daughters. It was the sort of joke that would have appealed to him.

As Lise felt drawn to the kitchen, Kate felt drawn to her father's desk. While still in Brackwede, she had learned to use his typewriter. One day he brought three callers to see her at it, just at the moment when – making a list – she was typing a row of dots. 'That's easy enough to do,' one of them commented, leaving her deeply offended. And who did he think had typed out all the rest?

In her last five years at home, when her father's office was also their sitting-room, she often helped him to make blueprints. The large heavy frame had to be taken on to the balcony to be exposed to the light until the sheet receiving the drawing (made on transparent paper) had turned the right shade of pink. It was then desensitized and rolled up in a box containing an eye-stinging spirit – a process which also needed to be timed by colour.

Paul interpreted the evidence to suit his hopes: Kate was going to become an architect, or perhaps what one of his granddaughters, who was to inherit his talent, in her earliest years called 'a drawer and painter'.

Towards the end of her first term in the Sarepta school, at assembly one morning the headmaster announced a competition, open to the whole school, for a poster advertising the summer fête to be held on a site beyond Brackwede, where there were pine forests and miles upon miles of heath.

Kate had the weekend in which to do it. It had to be her own unaided work, but of course they discussed it within the family. She should not draw a picture, which was what most people would do – this from Anne. The simplest posters were the most effective, Selma said. The words she used, COME TO THE SUMMER FETE, were Kate's choice. Paul sat her down at his desk, in front of his drawing-board.

She could not stop him from doing the measuring for her so as to place the letters evenly. He showed her how to make them stand out boldly by drawing their shadows only, in black *conté*. 'Show me on here,' Kate said, interposing scrap paper. She wanted to win too much, to be willing to risk being disqualified for having had help.

When the lettering was finished she felt that it was her father's work more than her own. Though her hand had done it, the idea had been his and he had told her, at every step, how to carry it out. He urged her to do nothing else to it, and turned his back on her, both actually and metaphorically, when she insisted on decorating it at random with small insects and the heads of flowers done in colour.

On Monday morning, the posters which had been entered – about two dozen – were exhibited in the school entrance hall. Anne said that she had overheard people debating whether or not a first former could have done Kate's poster, and concluding that only a first former could have spoiled such effective lettering in such a childish way.

Kate got her first prize, a pocket book on butterflies; she was called on to the podium in front of the whole school to receive it. She knew that she had had more help from her father than the rules allowed, and that therefore she ought not to have won. But whenever any endeavour of hers was rewarded she could always think of some reason why it ought not to have been.

Six

Paul was, like Kate, a third child. He had three brothers and a sister, all living in or around Berlin, but next to no contact with them. He used to say, 'They're afraid that I might ask them for money.' It sounded like one of his jokes but there was truth behind it. They were all better off than he, and after his father's death there had been some disagreement over his share of the inheritance.

The family estate had passed to Bernhard, the eldest. Once, so many years before that even Anne's recollection of it was vague, he and his wife had passed through Bielefeld on their way to a spa, and had broken their journey for long enough to meet the family over lunch in a restaurant. They had no children. Selma said of Tante Paula, 'At first she didn't want them, and then she found that she had left it too late.'

Onkel Bernhard and Tante Paula died in the Holocaust.

Early in 1934, Tante Paula wrote to Selma that she would like to provide her three daughters with a holiday. 'But as I'm not used to children,' she wrote, 'I should prefer you to send them to me one at a time.'

'Why is she suddenly inviting us?' the girls asked.

'Perhaps she thinks that the time has come for us Jews to help each other,' their mother answered. She must have swallowed her pride for the sake of her daughters and prompted her.

With their thank-you letters, she enclosed one of her own, asking if perhaps at least the two younger ones could be invited together: it was the youngest who needed the holiday most and she was inseparable from the sister next to her in age.

She must have omitted to name them. Nothing about Anne except her crabbed handwriting betrayed the chaos within her; her letter was also the worst judged by its contents because she found it hardest to put herself under an obligation to anyone. Such strangers were her nieces to their aunt that she got their hierarchy wrong, assuming the youngest to be the eldest, a mistake resented by Kate who saw it more as an insult to Anne than as a compliment to herself.

Anne went to Eberswalde for two weeks of the Easter school holidays and she and Tante Paula enjoyed each other's company. 'I congratulate you,' Paula wrote to Selma – her letter sounded as if she believed that Selma needed to be told what to think of Anne. 'Now that I know what your daughters are like,' she wrote, 'I look forward tremendously to having the other two with me.' She seemed not to realize that only Anne could be expected to be like Anne. Lise and Kate thought this a great joke.

The Jewish Women's Association of Bielefeld had funds for sending needy Jewish children to holiday homes. In 1934 that slight girl with the big eyes, Kate Loewenthal, was at the top of their list. 'Would you like to go?' Selma asked her. 'It would mean going on your own – without Lise.'

It was the sort of surprise sometimes sprung on her at present-giving time: something she had not thought of at all turned out to be the very thing she most wanted. Ever since overhearing her mother telling the district medical officer that their separation would kill Kate, she had needed to prove to herself that she could survive without her mother. She also felt the need to tackle a reality not tempered for her by Lise.

Selma arranged for her to go with the first batch of children, so that she could afterwards go to Eberswalde with Lise and still be back in time to celebrate her eleventh birthday at home. She was sent to Salzuflen, which was not far away.

The group of six girls, of whom Kate was the youngest, included Hanne, Tante Hete's youngest, who like two of the others was Anne's age. She was not someone to look after Kate, as she was told to do when their mothers saw them off. Contact between the two families was so tenuous that Selma was much reassured by Hanne's presence.

Herr Wolff had been the chef of one of the spa's best hotels.

Dismissed from his job, he and his wife had turned their house into a children's home; this was their first season. Six boys from Hanover, aged ten and upward, were already installed. To utilize all the space, and perhaps to save money, the accommodation in the girls' dormitory included a child's cot. Kate did not want to sleep in it either. Brunhilde – who was to become their group leader when Lise and Kate joined the Zionists the following year, by which time she had changed her name to Batya – made them all line up to demonstrate to Kate that she was the shortest.

Gisela, also, was someone whom Kate had not known before but took to on sight, chiefly because she had Lise's colouring. She was the one who had consented to pair off with Kate on the long walk from the station; she had even held hands. (Perhaps they were the only two charity children, something of which Kate was young enough to be oblivious.) The cot stood right up against one of the double beds and to reconcile Kate to it, Gisela offered to sleep next to her. Kate believed this to be a true *mitzvah* – the sort of good deed with which a Jew who believes in God strives to earn grace. On going to sleep and on waking up, it comforted Kate in her homesickness more than Gisela knew: by only half looking at the black hair and the brown eyes, she could pretend to herself that that was Lise. Gisela always lay facing Kate; like Lise she still sucked her thumb, she must not have wanted anyone else to know it.

Salzuflen became a spa because its water contains mineral salts. In the parks there were house-high thorn hedges down which the water was sent percolating; it had over the years built up a white deposit which scented the air. The children were taken to sit on nearby benches to get the benefit of it, and they were taken to the pump-room to drink the water. A daily bath in it was prescribed for some, but not for Kate, who needed building up.

Explaining this on one of the postcards they were expected to write home, she made a spelling mistake which meant that she had written not that the salt-air took it out of you but that it harassed you. It wasn't much of a joke but the others kept quoting it at her, because being made fun of drove her wild. Looking for a chance to retaliate, she browsed a day or two later among the cards waiting to be posted and found that Gisela – Gisela! – had written, 'Last night Kate farted in her sleep like thunder.' It embarrassed her horribly.

Herr Wolff was rightly proud of his cooking but it was unsuitable for children. Kate's digestion rebelled against it but it was to her taste. When given the chance, she overate even when happy. The pull of home, compounded by the urge to escape from being the butt of the other girls, made her make the most of the one thing she liked about being where she was: for more than a year now she had often gone hungry. She was always the first to ask for a second helping. Herr Wolff held her appetite up as an example to the others; he joked with her that she was eating to please him.

Wearing his chef's hat, he sat down on the couch and patted the space next to him, for 'the cook's pet' to come and sit there. When she did, he put his arm about her. She often felt that she had had more than enough of being cuddled by her mother, but she craved being cuddled in her homesickness. He told her that it was a great grief to him that his wife had not wanted children and that what he wished for most was to have a daughter like her.

He brought his large hand down over her far shoulder until the tip of his middle finger rested against her nipple. She believed that being cuddled was what felt so good. And also, she was too full of food to move.

They had arrived on a Friday. On the following Wednesday, unexpectedly and unannounced, some of the mothers, including Selma, turned up to see how their daughters had settled in. It was a fantasy-mother Kate had been homesick for – or so it felt to her once her mother was there. She felt – perhaps for the first time – a little ashamed of Selma, so fat and dowdy; but it was not that. She felt more ashamed of herself for having so missed her, who wasn't anyone special. She was convinced that she over-estimated her mother: nobody else thought of her as much as she did, or needed her as much, except Lise – and Lise didn't count. Anne (Kate believed) did not love their mother as much. Anne was self-sufficient and would not have missed her so.

With Selma there, Kate did not miss Anne and Lise, and that convinced her that it was not them she had missed, that she had not missed them at all. She was used to the feeling of missing her father even when he was there, because even when he was present he was most of the time, metaphorically speaking, beyond her reach.

Selma was horrified to learn that Kate slept in a cot. And because of Kate's complex emotions about her, instead of grabbing the chance to be taken home, she sprang to the defence of the Wolffs and said that it was all right, that she didn't mind. (She knew that she had not been homesick because she had only a cot to sleep in.) She did not want her mother to make a fuss. Above all, she did not want her to *know* because that would have upset her. She did not want to provide the other girls with ammunition against her by allowing them to witness her and her mother in each other's arms, weeping. This explains why Kate behaved as if she were happy. It did not make her happy to have her mother there.

Selma told Kate that she had come as Tante Hete's guest. She did not want to have her fare paid by her a second time, and they themselves could not really afford it – so would Kate mind, she asked her, if she did not come again on the Sunday, when Tante Hete would be coming again and no doubt more parents would come? Would Kate prepare herself for seeing the other girls receiving visitors and having none herself?

'I'll find the money somehow if you tell me that you want me to come,' her mother said. Kate did not want her to come again. While her mother was there she believed she did not want her, but she could not make herself say this, not out of politeness but because she knew that the words would have precipitated tears. Instead, she assured her mother that she was all right, there were only two and a half more weeks to go.

The surname of one of the boys was Israel. With astonishment, Kate listened to Brunhilde telling him that he was to be envied for it. (Her own was Kratzer.) With such a name, Kate thought, everyone would know instantly that you were a Jew. Hanne and some of the other girls enjoyed telling Kate when she tried to join in that it wasn't her conversation; not Brunhilde, she was a born youth leader. And so Kate told her what she was thinking and she answered, 'What's wrong with being known to be a Jew? It's something to be proud of.'

Kate knew that that had been her Opa's opinion; she took it for granted that prison would have changed it for him, that it would have been changed further by all that had happened since. Her father might not be ashamed of being a Jew, as she was, but neither was he proud of it (she believed). If her mother was not ashamed of being a Jew, Kate felt that she ought to have been. To Lise it was something she had to suffer for the sake of the world – which was the sort of pronouncement to make Kate ashamed of Lise. In Kate's opinion, only Anne need not be ashamed of being a Jew because she was Anne.

Brunhilde's father had been born in Poland. Her family were the sort of Jews, Kate had overheard Selma saying, who were the cause of German anti-Semitism. Kate therefore thought that maybe Brunhilde was right as far as she was concerned. If it was better to be a German Jew than a Polish one, it might be better to be a Jew than a Pole. But Kate would have preferred, very very much so, then and for some time to come, not to have been a Jew at all but an Aryan.

It was Brunhilde's idea to prepare an entertainment for the parents who were coming on the Sunday. It must have been, for even the farce they put on was Zionist propaganda. Kate refused to be cast in it. She doubted her own worth too much to be willing to pretend to be someone whom people would laugh at. It was not the stage but the back-stage which drew her. She would always be too unsure of her identity to be willing to pretend she was someone else. But with her passion for make-believe and her craving to be someone who mattered, being behind the scenes was what suited her to perfection.

Brunhilde was more interested in her than Kate knew. Brunhilde wanted to make a Zionist of her, not because she especially liked Kate but because she believed that that was what all Jews should be. And perhaps she did not want her to be left out because she expected her mother to come again.

To Kate she allocated the task of entertaining the audience during a necessary interval. She was to tell a story about Moses as a child at Pharaoh's court. While she chose the right words – without writing them down – and memorized them, Kate forgot to be homesick; she was even enjoying herself.

The following Sunday – not quite one more week to go – the spa staged its annual celebrations. There were to be fireworks in the evening, and a band would be playing in the central park. For days beforehand it was talked of as a great treat. It was the sort of thing Selma called *goyen nakhes* – a patronizing word meaning something which only Gentiles would find entertaining. It made Kate believe that she ought not to like it but she rather suspected that she would.

This inner conflict in addition to all the others was too much for her. On their outings, she had overheard one of the boys telling the others that he had just had his appendix out. She had chosen, one day, to walk with him so that she could question him about it; she was interested in that sort of thing. Having been constipated for some days and finding this too embarrassing to mention, on the day of the celebrations she decided to make believe that she had appendicitis. It was late afternoon before she had worked up sufficient conviction about it to make the Wolffs take notice.

'You would!' Frau Wolff said, with no sympathy whatsoever for Kate, whose pains were real enough. Subliminal jealousy made them detest each other.

Herr Wolff told Kate to show him where it hurt, and massaged her tummy. His irrelevant tenderness brought tears to her eyes. He would take her to the doctor, he decided, while his wife took the other children into town.

The children's home's doctor was Bernhard Loewenthal, one of her father's cousins. She had not met him before coming to Salzuflen, so little contact did Paul have with his relations. To Kate, being able to call him uncle was a privilege which mattered because it singled her out. Going to him was the next best thing to returning home. It was only a short walk.

After questioning her about her symptoms, her uncle bade her lie down and palpated her tummy. 'Yes,' she said truthfully when it hurt. Her father's father and uncle Bernhard's father had been brothers; the family resemblance she could see or imagined seeing was sufficient to aggravate both her homesickness and her feeling of guilt about trying to deceive him. He growled, now and then, and before long he said, 'Appendicitis.'

It bewildered her. Never before, no matter how hard she had tried, had she succeeded in making herself fall ill – perhaps he was just a bad doctor. Appendectomies were very common in those days, and the thought of having the operation did not worry her. She was quite willing to suffer in exchange for being cosseted and getting presents.

He told her to stay as she was, lying down, while he telephoned her parents. She could hear him speaking in the next room, but could not make out what he said. Herr Wolff came to her side, took her hand, looked down at her lovingly and said, 'We shall look after you.' He meant himself and his sour wife.

Her uncle came back and explained that he had spoken to her mother. He had offered to look after her himself, in his own home, before and after the operation. But her parents had decided to come and fetch her. They would be there within a couple of hours.

Her uncle's wife was dead. He had a daughter a little older than Kate; they had met only on the one occasion when all the girls had come to be measured and weighed. That evening she was out, watching the festivities. Kate envied her a little for having had her father all to herself.

She had begun to feel better. Given the chance she would have said that now she was all right. Now that she knew she was about to go home, she was rather sorry not to have waited until the next day before complaining of stomach ache, which was a pain she was used to. Her uncle made her sit in an armchair, with a blanket about her and his housekeeper brought her a cup of chicken soup.

Herr Wolff allowed himself to be persuaded to leave; in fact he seemed to be glad to be going. Not until years later did Kate understand what it was that she might have told her parents about him – all that cuddling – which had made him reluctant to face them.

Left by herself with the light dimmed, Kate slept; it was past her bedtime. She awoke to the sound of familiar voices and at that moment, if she had been required to pay for the reunion with a limb, she would have been willing.

It was less than a year since she had almost died. Her parents had had a fright but the sight of her reassured them. They were faced with a practical problem: when they had got to the station in Bielefeld they had discovered that there was no train back.

'I would take you in my car,' her uncle said, 'but there's something wrong with the clutch, I doubt it could make the journey.' They were welcome to stay the night, he suggested. They could not do that because of their other daughters.

On that day Salzuflen was crowded with visitors. Cars were parked all along the curbs bumper to bumper. They wrapped Kate up in the blanket and Paul carried her out into the brightly lit windy streets to find someone who had driven from Bielefeld and was ready to return there (by now it was close to midnight), who had the space and was willing to take them. 'Sorry, no,' people who were not able to take them said, or just, 'No' if they were anti-Semites who recognized them as Jews. Eventually, they came across a young man with a red sports car. It would be very cold for them, he said. He even agreed to wait ten minutes to give them the chance to hitch a more suitable lift. They failed to do so.

Goethe's *Erlkönig* tells of a father who rides through the night with his sick son in his arms; the boy dies just as they arrive home. Schubert's setting of the poem was well known to both Selma and Kate. Throughout the journey it was on their minds but each refrained from mentioning it to the other.

Dr Griesbach, who came in the morning, did not believe in cutting away what nature had provided, which was why Kate still had her tonsils. He had said that she needed them to guard her stomach. He questioned her about what she had been eating and shook his head.

There was nothing much wrong with her – after half a night in her own bed, with Anne as good as between her and the window and Lise as good as between her and the door, and her mother and father within call.

If Kate felt that she could not survive away from home, Selma must have thought, then the best thing for her was to be sent away again. Eberswalde was a lot further, but the people there were relations; she must have been reassured by what Anne had told her about them. Above all, Kate would have Lise.

They went for a fortnight, and if they did not altogether like it, this had nothing to do with being away from home.

On sight, they were a disappointment to their Tante Paula, who had come to Berlin to meet their train. They were grubby after their four-hour journey, they were tongue-tied and bashful, but she saw them exchanging what she thought were impudent glances. 'You aren't very like your sister Anne,' was one of the first things she said.

They did not mind that: they knew and regretted it. Far more than their aunt could do they wished that they were more like Anne. They might have warmed to her in spite of her make-up and her elegant clothes, had she not then said, 'Shame on your mother for letting you be so thin!' Throughout their stay they had to put up with aspersions cast on their mother which sounded to them as if their aunt believed that should she choose to compete in mothering them, she would be the winner.

They did not come to their mother's defence. That, they believed, would have been an insult to her; she was above needing to be defended. They thought it stupid of their aunt to make such comments; it made them wary of her, unwilling to make the allowances which their mother had told them to make because she had no experience with children. (Anne was always so far ahead of them that at no stage did they think of her as a child: since this was the term for them, it did not apply to her.)

Tante Paula gave the impression of wanting to come between them and their mother also by insisting on supervising their letters home. That very first evening, she made them write to say that they had arrived – after telephoning herself. 'Mutti knows,' they argued. For them to write was no more than polite, their aunt said. They were used to relating to their mother in whatever way they did not because it was expected of them but because they loved her. They had only just left and had nothing to say, except about Tante Paula – such things as could not be written down while she was standing over them to correct their spelling mistakes. As if these could have detracted from the value their letters would have for their mother! She prompted them what to write, dictated the words to them. They worried in case their mother thought something was wrong because their letters sounded so unlike themselves.

In their efforts not to lay themselves and their mother open to criticism, they behaved worse than they did at home. Summoned to eat, for instance, they came to the table without having washed their hands, so as not to keep their aunt waiting. Wishing to be polite, they said, 'Yes, please,' to everything she suggested for their entertainment, until she said that they should do none of it, to teach them not to be greedy. She didn't mean it; she wanted them to be happy with her – on her terms. She said, 'If it weren't for your sister Anne, I wouldn't think much of your mother's way of raising daughters. But as it can't be her fault that you're the way you are it must be your own.'

If only so as not to shame their mother or spoil Anne's chances of being invited again (she never was), they would have liked to have pleased her. But often they simply did not know what she expected of them. To her, much of their natural behaviour was naughty: coming in by the front door, for instance, or sitting down in the daytime on one's bed. 'Tante Paula *darf das*' (is allowed to do this) they took back to Bielefeld as a family saying. They thought it absurd to have adults and children living together according to different rules.

Their Onkel Bernhard, in appearance and manner, did not resemble their father much, but sufficiently so to make them feel at home with him. He allowed them the run of the stables, barns, orchards, and paddocks. He taught them to ride Maya, the elderly mare which had served with him in the cavalry throughout the Great War. He took them out in the landau and let them hold the reins; he took them out in his car and sat them, one at a time, on his knees to let them steer. Their aunt disapproved of whatever it was she saw him doing with them, and stopped it.

Like their mother, Tante Paula slept or rested for two hours after lunch. She expected them, if they stayed in, to keep quiet, and not to get themselves dirty if they went out. One day, bored, they wandered off and discovered that there was a fair. They had no money. A stall-holder invited Kate to have a free go: she threw a ball and won another go. She was not normally skilful and he must have been making use of her so as to attract others, but it made Kate believe herself to be lucky, then and for years to come. Lise, partly to get her away from there, drew her attention to the smoke that was rising from within the forest.

As a matter of course they went in search of it. Further and further in among the trees they went, until they had gone so far that it seemed absurd to them to turn back without having found what they had come for, yet they knew that they were staying out much too long. Feeling uneasy all the while because they had gone off without permission, they were not even enjoying themselves. They had still not found the fire when the sun dropped behind the trees.

Their aunt was waiting for them on the doorstep, very angry. 'How dare you!'

They knew that she was right to scold them, but they tried to excuse themselves, and explained that they had not asked for her permission to go off because they had not wanted to disturb her. They had had the choice of remaining at home, she pointed out. But a forest fire! they argued, making things worse, not better. Well-brought-up little girls, she said, were not interested in things like that.

Telling them that they looked like gypsy children – faces and hands stained by the forest and their dresses torn – she sent them to take a bath (together, as they always did at home, where they did so to save on the hot water). 'And then straight into bed without supper!' They knew what their mother thought of people who withheld food from children and/or sent them to bed as a punishment.

She didn't mean it. She came to see that they washed between their legs, and told them to come downstairs in their dressing-gowns. There and then they should write and tell their mother of their naughtiness. Lise and Kate grinned at each other; certain of their mother's understanding, they felt both superior to and sorry for their aunt.

She said that as a punishment she would not take them to the Berlin Zoo. But she did not mean this either, she had been looking forward too much to the pleasure of taking them. It was to be the climax of their stay and she had already bought them new dresses for this outing, strawberry pink with a pattern of white rings and spots. Selma was beginning to have to clothe them in cast-offs provided by the Jewish community. They would have been pleased to have had new dresses, had their aunt not commented that it was remiss of their mother to pack nothing in which they were fit to be seen, and said to Lise, trying on the new dress, that she looked like a scarecrow because the puffed sleeves accentuated the thinness of her arms.

She got too much satisfaction out of feeding them to withhold their supper. In spite of the two servants she could still afford to keep, she did all her own cooking. 'Is Tante Paula a better cook than your mother?' she asked. They thought the question unfair. No doubt Anne would have – must have – found a diplomatic answer to it. The truth was that she was, but they preferred their food plain. Even Kate did, so soon after Salzuflen.

One day when they were playing in the orchard, she called them to the kitchen window for their mid-morning snack. No need for them to bring dirt into the house – she had cooked them something they could eat out of their hands. *Kremslach*: matzo-meal pancakes with a sprinkling of cinnamon. They had never had those before and they liked the taste. They said so and their aunt cooked them two more, and another two. They were too rich for the girls to go on eating them, but when they tried to refuse, she said, 'Go on, I won't think you greedy!' They feared to offend her by admitting that they were beginning to feel sick. The next two *kremslach* were both eaten by Lise, but then even she could barely manage one more. Kate buried hers under one of the apple trees.

When their aunt had finished cooking *kremslach*, she came out for a stroll. She had a black lap-dog called Muschi. Muschi dug up the buried pancake. With the sand sticking to it, it looked like a rusty tin lid. Tante Paula exclaimed, 'That's not fit for a little dog to eat!' and Kate took it away from him, quickly, so that she wouldn't find out what it was.

Kate and Lise thought it an excellent joke, and liked their aunt better for having enabled them to laugh at her.

The only one of Paul's siblings to escape the Holocaust was his sister Ina. Her husband, Wilhelm Michaelis, was sent after the *Kristallnacht* to Oranienburg concentration camp, which made total strangers make the effort necessary to get him and his family out of Germany.

Seven

The synagogue in Bielefeld had been built at the beginning of the century, with seating for eight hundred people. By the time Hitler came to power, the congregation numbered almost a thousand. On the High Holy Days, when everybody attended, women and girls sat up in the balconies. At other times the women sat downstairs in the main part on the right, and the girls in the right aisle. The pews were of dark-stained oak. The stone floor was covered with red coconut-matting. In front was a stone balustrade and on it, at each end, a large candelabrum with lights looking like candles. Behind this was the dais, with the altar, and on either side, two unobtrusive benches. When they were not participating in the service, the rabbi sat on the left side, the cantor on the right.

On either side behind the altar, steps led up to the shrine, its double doors concealed behind a curtain. This was a rich community, possessing many scrolls, each decked with silver ornaments exchanged for gold ones on festivals, when all the silver-embroidered blue-velvet hangings were exchanged for ones of shot white silk embroidered with gold thread. Behind the shrine rose the massive pipes of the synagogue organ, proclaiming these Jews to be liberal, as did the stained glass windows and the cupola, painted night-sky blue with gold stars, with a surround of a blessing in Gothic Hebrew script. On the outside, four small domed towers echoed the central dome with its Star of David, which rose above all the church spires of the town.

Kate and her sisters were still living in Brackwede when, on the death of the old cantor, the community engaged, for the sake of his glorious voice, a man so young that he had only just qualified. Siegfried Friedemann. He was generally referred to as Friedemann,

'Herr' being too respectful and 'Siegfried' too intimate. Selma referred to him as Friedchen, trivializing the feelings she had about him, which were shared by other Jewish matrons without sons and with growing daughters. He said to her, once when she gently teased him about his bachelor state, 'I'll wait till one of your daughters is old enough.' Kate happened to be standing there with them, and he was looking at her.

The Jews of the district flocked, as if it were Yom Kippur, to his early performances. Afterwards, Lise and Kate walked on the windy hillside, the grass standing high, and improvised a song.

> *At what pace shall I walk from the vestry to the altar, that is the question.*
> *What shall I look at as I walk, that is the question.*
> *What shall I do with my hands as I walk, that is the question.*

Thus they tried to express the emotions aroused in them by the phenomenon of one so young and accessible being the go-between between them and God. What they felt for him could not have been love of the usual sort – they were only ten and nine years old. Whatever it was, with Kate the feeling outlasted her childhood.

There had not been a Jewish school in Bielefeld for more than fifty years. Jewish children received twice weekly instruction from the cantor, in the afternoon, on Mondays in Jewish history and on Thursdays in liturgical Hebrew, which differs from modern Hebrew slightly in pronunciation. Until the mid-thirties, these classes were held in one or another of the town's schools, and after that in the community building adjoining the synagogue. For older children, the rabbi held a Bible class after Saturday morning service.

When Friedemann first took up his post, there was talk of having him come out once a week to teach the children in Brackwede – meaning the three granddaughters of the president of the community. It was one of the things Lise and Kate prayed for. But nothing had yet come of it when Hitler took power.

When they began to attend after moving to Bielefeld, Friedemann held his classes in one of the girls' high schools near the centre in an ancient, romantic backwater of the town, frequented only by those who belonged to it – or so it felt to Kate: the old stones demanded a tithe of affection when you walked there.

The school, when you entered, felt deserted; you had to brave the dark dreary corridors and stairs, your echoing footfall proclaiming your presence, past many closed doors to the one which stood open, allowing the sound of familiar voices to guide you to it. Lise and Kate did not like to be the first, but neither did they like to be the last. They wished to be there when Friedemann arrived, out of consideration for him and so as not to miss a moment of his presence. The sight of him had on them the effect of sudden hot sunshine. (Anne attended a more senior class.)

He was of medium height, lithe, with dark-blond wavy hair. He had a habit of running his fingers through it in moments of perplexity, which were many, causing a lock to fall forward over his exceptionally high forehead. His eyes were the blue of spring flowers. His features, his hands, were evidence of a sensitive nature. He was easily discomposed: the more forward girls competed in making him blush, which he did comprehensively, down his neck and up over his ears. Friedemann blushing was a spectacular sight. It made Kate sit even more still and quiet, so much so that one day he asked Selma, 'Your youngest, is she a little retarded?'

It was the result of Kate not wanting to add to the problems he had in keeping the class under control.

One day – it must have been in 1935 – the children were so rowdy that he gave them an imposition: to copy a page of Hebrew text. Perhaps a friend had suggested it to him – normally he did not even give them homework. Kate, with her craving for recognition, would have liked him to have said publicly that she need not do it, since she had contributed nothing to the noise beyond telling people to sit down and be quiet. Friedemann had not tried to quieten them; if she had been Anne she would have suggested that he bring his violin. As always, he took no notice of her, not even when all the others had left and they were, for a moment, alone.

Not doing the imposition would not have been the way to make an impression; she expected nobody else to do it and she was right. The Hebrew alphabet which they had been taught to write was a stylized version of the printed one, but there is a cursive way of writing the letters which is much more difficult. Kate learned it and used it to do her imposition.

'I'm not able to read this,' Friedemann said when she handed him the page on the steps of the synagogue before the lesson. (The builders were in the community rooms, making alterations upstairs where there was to be a café for Jews, no longer allowed to enter any other.) 'Where did you learn to write like this?' Friedemann asked, but instead of waiting for her answer (as always, Kate was tongue-tied in his presence) he added, 'I was walking behind you just now – you don't hold yourself straight enough. You walk along as if you were looking for something.'

She walked with downcast eyes looking for something that was not to be found on the pavement.

After the move back to town, all three girls were old enough to join the leisure activities beginning to be provided by the Jewish community for its children, in response to the growing discrimination.

Anne talked of becoming a Zionist, but only so as to reject the idea. She was more German than Hitler who was an Austrian, she said. It was her life and it was up to her to decide where to live it; if she were to go to Palestine it would be because she wanted to go there and not because the Nazis didn't want her in Germany. No one at that time believed that the rest of the German people would allow the Nazis to do as they wished with the Jews.

Paul told his daughters to join the German Jewish Youth, an offspring of the Association of Jewish Ex-Servicemen. Lise and Kate went to a few of their meetings to please their father, but felt uncomfortable about declaring themselves to be Germans. Lacking Anne's self-assurance, they were prompted by a different sort of pride, which would not allow them to wish to remain where they were not wanted.

The older generation of the Jews of Bielefeld would have nothing to do with Zionism. 'It plays right into Hitler's hands,' they argued, 'by maintaining that we have another homeland.' They could not stop those in their late teens and early twenties from joining the Zionist movement and some of them even emigrating to Palestine. But they fought against Zionist ideas spreading to the younger age groups. The most they would allow was the formation of the Maccabi sports club. Lise and Kate joined it. Anne didn't; she didn't like sport and argued that an exclusively Jewish club was also racist. Its uniform was white and the shade of blue of the Israeli flag, its badge included Hebrew lettering and the Star of David.

At first it met on Monday evenings in the gymnasium of Kate's old elementary school just off Kügler Street; later it met in one of the high schools, where there was sports apparatus to be used by the older groups. Lise and Kate then discovered that if they stayed on after their own session until it was the turn of the young adults, they would see Friedemann is singlet and shorts, being athletic.

They continued to be allowed to use the gym until after Kate became pubescent. Lise was too thin to develop breasts, which made Kate's own of greater than usual importance. Being the one thing she had which Lise hadn't, they made her value herself a little more.

The sports club was still meeting in its first venue, and Lise and Kate still belonged to its youngest age group, when these children were told one evening to stay on until the end, when an important announcement was to be made. Several of the children objected that their mothers would worry if they didn't come home at the usual time. Lise and Kate said that they lived only just down the road; couldn't one of them run home and tell their mother? 'You must all stay,' they were told. 'One of the things young Jews have to learn is discipline.'

This putting of the communal purpose above the interests of the individual was what, after they had left Germany, tore Lise away from Kate, each to live on as a solitary survivor almost as if the other had died.

The announcement was that from now on, the Maccabi sports club was to be affiliated to the Maccabi Hatzair, a somewhat left-wing Zionist youth organization. All membership had been automatically cancelled; those who still wished to belong needed to rejoin. They were told to think it over; Lise and Kate made up their minds at once. It felt good to them to be members of a group and they welcomed the idea of eventually going to live in a country which not merely wanted but needed them.

They belonged to the youngest group, called the Chicks and led by

Batya – the Brunhilde who, the previous year, had been with Kate in Salzuflen.

Until the local Jewish council relented and allowed them to use the community rooms, the group, averaging an attendance of ten, met in one or another of the homes of its members – usually of those who lived fairly centrally and whose fathers were still earning, whose mothers would provide lemonade and little bowls of mixed almonds and raisins. They never met in Batya's home, not because her parents were separated, nor because the family was poor, but because it was Polish. Some of the Chicks' mothers, including Selma, still believed that the Nazis would make a distinction between the Jews of East European origin and 'us Germans'.

They met on Wednesday afternoons, partly because none of Friedemann's classes happened to be held then, but chiefly because that was when the HJ and BDM (the Hitler Youth and its girls' equivalent) met. Some Jewish children, including for a while Kate but never Lise, would have preferred to belong to the Nazi organizations; few adults and fewer children as yet understood their true purpose. The HJ and the BDM were taught to see themselves as an élite and that was how the rest of the population, including the ineligible Jewish children, saw them.

The young Zionists sought compensation by copying all they envied: the wearing of a uniform, the rallies with their sing-songs around camp fires. At weekends, they too marched behind flags through the forest and across the heath. They did it to modern Hebrew songs as well as to the traditional German ones, thus scoring by having two cultures to draw on. Another difference was that they left the town by tram in twos and threes, with nondescript wind jackets over their blue and white, their pennon in somebody's pocket. Excluded from the town's sports fields, the Jews had their own on the far side of Brackwede.

Batya's emigration, at the end of 1935, to a kibbutz in the Land of Israel, made her not less but more important to Kate, who wrote her long letters, extravagantly long. By means of these she learned to put her ideas into words on paper. She had not especially liked Batya, their relationship had not been close. Batya did not write back and

Kate eventually stopped writing to her. What made her persist for so long was not only the need for self-expression but also the thought of her ideas arriving – like homing pigeons – in the Land of Israel.

Under the leadership of Lotte, the Chicks were renamed *Devorah*, Hebrew for bee. Lise and Kate took on the task of making a new pennon. Lise cut it out and did the seams; Kate drew the bee and the Hebrew lettering; between them, they did the embroidery.

'What do you think is the meaning of our new name?' Lotte asked the group, and after a moment, when nobody else spoke up, Lise answered, 'As the bee produces honey, we Jews produced the Bible, and others took it away from us and put it to their own use.' Kate wished she had thought of that answer.

Within the family, Lise was considered stupid, if only by comparison with her sisters. But she sometimes made Kate intensely jealous by coming out with things which made Selma say, 'It shows that you have rabbis among your ancestors.' For instance, when Anne argued that Darwin had proved that the world could not have been created in six days, Lise said, 'It says in the Bible that to God, a thousand years are like one day, and that is the explanation.' She was not repeating something she had read or heard.

Kate was not yet twelve when Friedemann started a children's choir for the synagogue services. He tried to exclude her from it on the grounds that she was too young. At the end of his lessons that week he had asked all who wanted to become members to come to the synagogue that Friday evening half an hour before the service, to talk about it. Lise and Kate turned up as a matter of course, with ten or so other children.

'Only people from the age of twelve,' he said, once they had ranged themselves on the benches beside the organ. He may not have known or remembered how old Kate was but she was the smallest child there, and he was looking at her – without seeing her as she was. 'The younger ones aren't yet sensible enough.' Perhaps he was quoting someone, perhaps Dr Kronheim, the rabbi.

'But Kate is very sensible!' the meek Lise instantly sprang to her defence. 'You know she is, you know her!' She was outraged.

Kate sat there like a moron, not even prompted to tears, she was so stunned.

Lise said, 'If Kate can't come I won't either.' She loved to sing. They both loved being in the synagogue which, they felt, was the one place in Bielefeld where they had an unquestionable, an inalienable right to be – more so than in their own home, which was rented on a monthly basis from an Aryan landlord who could give them notice any time he chose. They loved the atmosphere in the synagogue, compounded of the solidity of the building and all the intangible thoughts and prayers people had had there. Being there made them feel touched with holiness, made them feel part of the tradition dating back to the Temple in Jerusalem, when the Jews were a heroic people – caught them up like pearls strung on a necklace. They had wanted to join the choir because of this.

He should allow Kate to come if she wanted to, the other children began to say, not because they wanted her there – they didn't care one way or the other – but for the sake of arguing with Friedemann, of asserting themselves and rebelling against him as they always did, perhaps because he personified for them the Jewishness which had begun to blight their lives.

And as always he gave in to them: Kate could stay as long as she behaved herself. It wasn't a victory as far as she was concerned. Anne was the only other person in her life who could have wounded her so deeply. How negligible she must be, she thought, that, loving him as much as she was capable of loving, she had after two years of attending his classes left no impression on him.

Oh, how she wished that day to have a voice like Lise's!

Fortunately for Kate, he did not test their musical abilities, feeling perhaps that beggars can't be choosers. He sat down at the organ and asked them to sing as he played one of the prayers with which they were familiar because it was traditionally sung by the congregation. Kate opened her mouth, of course she did, she did not want to give him cause to complain of her. And precisely for that reason she did not dare to make a sound.

From then on the adult choir, depleted by emigration which increased in the course of that year, sang only on Holy Days. For the Sabbath services – Friday night and Saturday morning – the children sang, praising God and thanking him for having created them Jews.

Eight

Until she was twelve years old, Kate believed that the damage done to her life by her Jewishness could be contained.

The school year finished at Easter. On the last day of term, when the teacher read out the names in order of merit before distributing the reports, Kate's came first and next came Ingrid's. Lore's name did not come until after people had stopped counting.

And when the class (now the second form) reassembled on the first school morning after the holidays, as they were all milling about catching up with each other's news – Kate standing by herself with no one to talk to – Ingrid sought her out to ask, 'Shall you and I sit together?'

Luck entered into it: in the course of the holidays, Ingrid and Lore had quarrelled. What about, Kate did not find out; she never became Ingrid's friend to the extent of exchanging real confidences. The friendship started promisingly enough but did not develop. Still, the first few weeks of that term were the happiest of Kate's school life. They were among the happiest weeks of her childhood.

Girls who were excused from gym watched from the balcony. Kate, having a cold, stood up there one day looking down upon Ingrid and thought, I love that girl. Afterwards, when she told Ingrid that it was easy to single her out because she had the brightest head of hair, the whitest skin, the trimmest body, Ingrid said that Kate was easy to single out, too, because her hair and her skin were the darkest, and that altogether she was 'as sweet as a kitten'. This praise of her did not matter to Kate as much as the knowledge that she was the one for whom Ingrid had looked out.

They must have appeared a striking pair: the sparkling Aryan and the sombre Jewess. No one except Ingrid could have got away with it as far as the rest of the class was concerned. Instead of causing Ingrid's downfall, the friendship raised Kate's standing and made her the adjutant to the queen of the class. This left her indifferent; with Ingrid as her best friend she needed nobody else. For a while it seemed as if Ingrid were content to have no other friends either.

Ingrid lived in one of the wealthy neighbourhoods known to Kate because the rabbi, Dr Kronheim, lived there. (Though by now, there was not a street in Bielefeld Kate and Lise had not walked through, as, in Brackwede, there was not a stretch of forest which they had not explored.) For the first few days of their friendship Kate caught the same tram home. Ingrid travelled no more than four stops but to Kate it was worth it. She was left with a mental afterglow as if Ingrid were abstract sunshine. It even penetrated her thick skin. 'At last you have some colour in your cheeks!' her mother said, and felt her forehead.

During her life, Kate often wished that she had not been born, but she did not wish it in those days.

She warned her mother, 'Don't worry if I'm late one of these days.' Expecting too much of life as always, she added, 'If I'm later than Papa, don't wait for me, I may be having lunch at a friend's house.'

The day came when Ingrid asked her to go all the way home with her.

There was a man-high hedge around the garden, and a slatted wooden fence around that. The gate was solid and had to be unlocked from within the house. The garden was large enough to include mature trees; the house was turreted. Kate got no further than the entrance hall, where, one day, Ingrid's father, in a benign manner, interrogated her. Either she managed to conceal that she was a Jew (the term of execration was never *Jüdin*, always *Jude*), or it did not bother him. Learning that Kate walked to school in the mornings, from a neighbourhood beyond theirs, he told his daughter not to be so lazy and instead of taking the tram get her friend to call for her, so that they could walk together.

It was a little out of Kate's way but she would have been willing to walk a lot further for the sake of securing Ingrid's company. It meant abandoning Lise; Kate felt so badly about leaving her to walk by herself that she offered to pay half her tram fare.

Having seen Ingrid home, Kate played ball with her in the garden. Ingrid had a sister two years younger, a pale copy of her, who joined in. One day their mother brought out glasses of lemonade. Had Kate not had such details to remember, she would have come to believe that her friendship with Ingrid was something she had only imagined.

Of course she knew that it could not last, that the times and time itself were against her. She thought herself better than Lore, but not by much. Perhaps Ingrid had set out only to use her to make Lore jealous – and either found Kate's company agreeable enough or she found Kate, after having encouraged her, difficult to get rid of. Or she may have wanted to prove to herself or to her classmates that she could make a friend of anyone. She may have wanted to demonstrate her independence, her ability to defy the rules of Hitler's Germany. She may even have done it for a bet. She was that sort of girl, like Anne.

There was too little warmth and too much constraint between them for even the self-deceiving Kate to believe that they had become truly best friends. Though Ingrid had not yet joined the BDM, too much of their lives existed in mutually exclusive spheres. But friends they were. When school broke up for the summer holidays, Kate would be going away and they promised to write to each other.

That summer, the Jewish Women's Association sent Kate to a children's home in the Taunus mountains beyond Frankfurt-on-Main. Given the choice when this was being arranged of how long to stay there, she unhesitatingly said, 'Four weeks', which was the most she was being offered. She always took as much as she could get, and she believed herself too old by now to suffer from homesickness – even on her twelfth birthday, for which she would still be there if she stayed that long. She was convinced that it was her mother's constant need to baby her that prevented her from being as independent as Anne.

Sisters of a Protestant nursing order – like those who had run the Bible class in Brackwede – on duty at railway stations, helped her to change trains in Dortmund and, in Frankfurt, to find the group of children with which she was to join up. They came from an orphanage in Cologne, enough of them to fill the home, making Kate the only outsider, and doubly so because they were orthodox. Not only that but most of the helpers in the home were also from the orphanage and so knew all the children, and all the children knew them, with the exception of Kate.

She told herself, this is the third, the third time that I've been away from home; I must, I must be getting used to it. But it was the first time that she was totally among strangers. They laughed at her for not knowing the rules by which they were used to living. They asked her, 'Are you sure that you are a Jew?' She allowed them to instruct her and she copied them. They were mostly younger than she, but even this did not tempt her to question or argue: what she wanted was to be able to feel that she belonged.

The orphans all took it for granted that she was an orphan too, if not from another institution then sent to the holiday home by guardians glad to be rid of her for a while. The story possibilities of this appealed to Kate, who was so addicted to stories, but having parents was not something about which to tell lies for fear that as a punishment they would come true. On the other hand, she did not think it right to mention home and parents to orphanage children. It would hurt them, and this would prejudice them against her as would her being more fortunate. And so she chose not to answer their questions about her background, making herself interesting to the others for a few days – until she got her first letter from home and somebody snatched it out of her hands while she was reading it.

The conclusion they drew was that she had been secretive because she thought herself better than they were. Three and a half weeks were not long enough for her to live this down.

The home, with space for thirty children, stood in its own large grounds on the afforested hillside above the small town of Rüdesheim. The setting reminded Kate of Brackwede. Twice daily, weather permitting, they went for walks two by two, holding hands. She was always one of the last to find a partner, someone else whom nobody wanted. They were allowed to break ranks once they got off the road. In the forest, Kate felt not merely at home but at an advantage over the townees, though strictly speaking she was a townee too. But living if only for three years in Brackwede had conditioned her for life.

Unlike the other children, she knew the names of the trees, bushes, flowers; when she didn't she made them up. When some adult knew better, she said, 'Well, that's what it's known as by us in Westphalia,' knowing that there was no one to contradict her. Gathering blackberries, she plunged into the brambles until her arms and legs were scratched and bleeding, her clothes purple-stained and torn. 'But Kate, there is no need,' the helper told her. There was for her: Kate, the forest expert, needed to be the first to fill her jam jar.

It had been wordlessly understood between her and her mother that this time, whatever her problems were she would cope with them by herself. She was anxious about the functioning of her digestion. That, and the different food, and more of it, and most of all her shyness about going to the lavatory – as if she were the only one who had this need – resulted in constipation. Three days, her mother had taught her, was the most one could safely go without defecating. She dared not wait to find out what would happen if then she did nothing about it.

Selma as a rule resorted to stewed figs or prunes. In Rüdesheim, Kate asked if she could have some and found herself among a group of candidates for receiving enemas – two boys and three girls. After their rest period, when the others assembled for the afternoon walk, they were told to stay behind. Everybody knew what for, and Kate found it horribly embarrassing. Yet such was her craving for individual attention that part of her was glad.

Dr Griesbach had prescribed an enema after Salzuflen, so she knew what to expect. There were two helpers, not much more than girls, perhaps they were nurses in training. The second one was there, the children heard, to hold them down. She would not need holding down, Kate averred, and was promptly taken first, praised for being so good, and held up to the others as an example. Off she went, from the dormitory to the lavatories, with clenched buttocks, and felt so much better afterwards that she considered it worth the embarrassment – though some of her relief must have been due to the ordeal being over.

It earned her smiles of recognition from the two helpers at every encounter; now they knew her by name. 'We need you to show the others how it's done,' they said, a few afternoons later. She told them that she was no longer constipated but they said that it would do her no harm. For the rest of her stay there they made use of her to demonstrate to other children that being given an enema was nothing to be scared of. 'Kate here volunteers for it,' they said, which was not true. She just didn't know how to defend herself against loving attention.

Her birthday fell five days before she was due to go home.

Selma made much of birthdays. Anne and Lise would find only a book by their place at the breakfast table if their birthday fell on a school-day. But Kate could count on getting all her presents first thing in the morning, festively displayed with cards and flowers on a white damask cloth. Lise's birthday fell two days after Anne's, but Kate's was not for another two months and two days. By a tradition dating from when she was too young to understand this, she always got one or two presents when the others got theirs – and by the time it came to her birthday these had ceased to count.

For something which Selma thought as essential as she did birthday presents, she always managed to find a little money which she made go a long way. She would trade in her daughters' outgrown toys and books, or one of the china ornaments she cherished. (She owned very little jewellery and household silver and these, with foresight, she held on to.) She scoured the shops and markets, especially on behalf of Kate, to whom the number of presents still mattered. She might even hold over, from December until August, the sort of thing on sale then to hang on a Christmas tree, for instance a shell containing folded paper, which under water blossoms out into a scene. Even a hair slide or ribbon, if at all special, would, wrapped up, make another present, or a set of pretty buttons to put on a passed-on dress.

Selma had warned Kate not to expect a parcel at Rüdesheim; they would be celebrating her birthday when she came home. She must have known that receiving a parcel through the post for the first time in her life would raise Kate's expectations to such a pitch that its contents, whatever it was, would be bound to disappoint. The birthday card and letter, to make certain that they would get there on time, had been posted too early and arrived the day before. All the letters from home always left Kate feeling disconsolate: it was as if the love waiting for her there were food which would spoil before she could get to it.

This was her first experience of being among people who did not know that the day was her birthday. She burned to mention it to someone, but asking for it would have made being congratulated worthless. And being twelve was such an important landmark! She did not realize that any other birthday would have mattered as much to her just because it did not matter to anyone she was with, just as she mattered to herself excessively without realizing it, and as a consequence of knowing how little she mattered to the rest of the world outside her family – and how little her family mattered to the rest of the world.

At tea-time there was a cake for her with pink candles. It came too late in the day, was no compensation and only embarrassed her.

If there was one thing Kate would have valued more than Ingrid's company it would have been a letter from Ingrid. She so valued the written word that this had been a factor in her calculations: if she stayed away for a whole four weeks, that would give her and Ingrid time to exchange some letters. (They would have been something tangible to comfort her once the friendship had come to an end.)

From the beginning, she waited for a letter from Ingrid more than she waited for a letter from home. Letters from home only confirmed that it wasn't the fault of the post that she had received nothing from Ingrid. She would have liked her to have been the first to write; it would have enhanced the letter's value. But she also wanted to spare her this miserable wait, and thought about her too much, with too much emotion, and liked writing letters too much to stop herself. She wrote as interestingly as she could, to make Ingrid glad to hear from her. But she also wrote, 'I miss you terribly', and, 'I count the days until I see you again'. She ended with, 'All my love always', meaning every word of it.

She received nothing from Ingrid.

Having waited a fortnight or so, she wrote again. She knew that she had to restrain herself in her letters home so that her mother wouldn't be anxious, but she needed to let herself go in writing and she did this to Ingrid, asking her, 'Why have you not written, why have you not answered me, what have I done wrong? Tell me, there must be some misunderstanding. Only write to me, you can tell me anything, you can count on me absolutely. Nothing will make any difference to how I feel about you. I love you. I shall always love you, you need do no more than accept it, I love you enough for us both.'

In the changing rooms of the sports ground used by the Sarepta school volley-ball team which met in the holidays, Ingrid read out that letter to some of their classmates.

Kate learned this from Grete, a hefty girl with a missionary background who had always been nice to her. Grete said, 'They all laughed at your letter and Ingrid made fun of you.'

Ingrid and Lore had been reconciled. On the first day of the new term, Ingrid changed places with the girl who had been sharing with Lore. She did it without saying a word about it to Kate, she did not speak to her at all, did not look at her. As far as she was concerned Kate had ceased to exist. She did not even think her worth her hostility.

It hurt and Kate did not know how to cope with it. She could avoid looking at Ingrid, avoid speaking to her, but she could not avoid her own emotions. She could not make herself accept what had happened; though expecting it, she was unprepared, had not known that it would come so soon and be so devastating. She continued to think that it could not really be true, not permanently so: Ingrid, who had changed her mind about Lore, twice, would change her mind about Kate. She persuaded herself that Ingrid was testing her. And so, her hopes renewed with each school-day, she bided her time. Else she could not have faced continuing to go to school – where some of the girls and also some of the staff had begun to turn up in Nazi uniform.

It was then the fashion to have an autograph album. In the days of their friendship Kate had given hers to Ingrid, who still had it. One morning when the opportunity arose, Kate asked her for its return. She did not care about the book – unless Ingrid had written in it; it was an excuse for her to talk to Ingrid, to convey to her that, as far as Kate was concerned, nothing had changed; and to provide Ingrid with an opening to change her attitude without loss of face.

92

Ingrid looked at her, looked through her, as if they had never walked with their arms about each other.

Having been overheard by Grete, or by someone who had told her, Grete said to Kate, 'I should like to write in your autograph book, shall I ask Ingrid for it?'

'There's no need,' Kate lied. 'She said she'd give it to me.' It was the one, the only link left between them.

Her isolation, now that she was no longer Ingrid's friend, seemed or perhaps was worse than before, not only by contrast but because even some of those who had previously associated with her now kept their distance, either in support of Ingrid or because they had meanwhile accepted the Nazi teaching concerning the Jews. During break-times Kate, reduced again to Lise's company, sought the edge of the playground, needing the feeling of having her back protected.

It was a frequent sight: Ingrid in the midst of their classmates, like a queen holding court. Then one day, she stepped forth from among them and walked towards Kate, all the others following her in a phalanx. She was holding Kate's autograph book. Handing it over, she said, 'I can't write in that, you must understand that I am a *German* girl.'

And am I *not* a German girl? Kate asked herself.

Nine

Anne's schooling ended when she was in the second term of the upper fourth, a few months after her fourteenth birthday. Her presence had long been irksome to several teachers because she would not tolerate injustices, whether affecting her classmates or historical figures. More than once, she was sent to the headmaster for insubordination, for instance over insisting that the words of that favourite German song, *Die Lorelei*, had been written by Heinrich Heine who, though baptized and therefore in his time not considered a Jew, had remained one according to the laws drawn up by the Nazis. 'Never mind,' the teacher had said. 'Sit down, Anne.' But she had remained standing and argued that if it was right to have burned his books then the song should be banned – or if it was still to be sung then it ought to be admitted that in the burning of Heine's books the Nazis had made a mistake. And if they were not infallibly right then perhaps . . .

She had already grown taller than Selma, had grown tall for a girl of her generation born in Germany into the post-war famine. She held herself always as if on parade; she marched rather than walked, so sure was she of herself – or wanted the world to believe that she was. Her hair was as coarse as Kate's and as black as Lise's. It was wavy and she wore it cut short enough to show her ear lobes. She trained one lock to fall across her forehead; it made her look challenging. Her skin was as white but not as delicate as Selma's, and full of freckles. Her nose neither grew too large, as Kate's was to do, nor Jewish-looking like Lise's. She did not, like them, inherit Paul's thin upper lip. Her waist fined down as her breasts filled out; her figure competed in beauty with her face. Her only blemish was her legs, which were too fat in the calves and ankles. Boys and men, even those wearing Nazi uniform, had begun to pay her attention. She pretended to ignore them all, but she and Selma exchanged on them the comments of connoisseurs.

One day that autumn, her class was told to come in on the Saturday for the purpose of collecting beech-nuts in the forest in aid of the Winter Relief Fund. Anne raised her hand and when called upon stood up and announced that, as a pacifist, she objected: because the money raised through that fund, ostensibly for the benefit of the poor, was – she wanted her classmates to know – spent by the government on rearmament.

The teacher did not argue the point but stated that the activity was compulsory. Anne always acted in keeping with her beliefs. On the Monday morning she was summoned by the headmaster.

She related, re-enacted at home what had happened. 'Why did you stay away?' he asked her, and she answered, 'Because collecting beech-nuts would have meant helping the Nazis to break international law.' She was referring to the Treaty of Versailles.

'As a Jew, you can't afford to fight this government,' the headmaster said and she answered, 'As a Jew, I can't afford to do anything else.'

He sighed, and asked her, 'If I tell you something in confidence, will you not repeat it – except of course to your parents?' The father of one of her classmates was a high-ranking Nazi, who objected to his daughter getting lower marks than a Jew. What, he asked Anne, was to be done about it? 'That's your problem,' Anne said, meeting his eyes until he looked away.

He waited, giving her time which she did not need, to think about it. Eventually, she asked him, 'How can you do something you cannot bring yourself to put into words?'

He said, 'Tell your father that I am profoundly sorry. But you leave me no choice.'

She said, 'I thought it was you who was running this school,' turned and marched out of his office.

It was still break-time. While she was speaking to Lise, the bell rang; to speak to Kate she called her out of her classroom. But all she said was, 'I wanted to tell you that I'm going home.' She must have felt just then that she needed her sisters; either she could not or she would not ask anything of them.

'What happened?' Kate asked, running after her down the wide staircase. At the foot of it stood the headmaster, waiting for Anne. 'My dear, don't be over-hasty, there is no need for your sisters . . .' He must have believed that she would take them away with her. But even her pride was less important to her than their schooling.

'Go back to your classroom,' the headmaster told Kate. He found it hard to take his eyes off Anne. 'Tell your teacher that you're late because I detained you.' Anne confirmed with no more than a look that she should do as told, and so Kate did, cheeks burning and feeling important.

But at the end of the lesson she raced to find Lise. What could have happened? they asked each other. Lise was the one who helped out: if their house were on fire, if their mother had fallen ill, it would have been she who was sent for. If anything had happened to their father, their mother would have sent for all or none of them. Their hearts in their throats, they went into the office and asked to be allowed to telephone home.

'You'll be going there anyway after the next lesson,' the secretary said, 'and then you'll be able to find out all you wish to know.' She was wearing a round enamel BDM badge, black, white and red, rather like the badges Lise and Kate possessed as owners of Göring-brand bicycles. But this one bestowed upon the wearer a charismatic authority.

After school they raced down the hill and caught the first possible tram, risked their lives changing quickly on the Jahnplatz, and felt as if they had still not caught their breath when they reached their stop. They ran all the remaining distance, Lise reining herself in to stay beside Kate.

That nothing as catastrophic as they had imagined had happened remained reassuring in the years ahead.

Anne said, 'It isn't as if I had been expelled. I left of my own accord.'

Anne talked of it as 'joining the Katag', but what it meant was that she went to work in a factory producing such things as shirts and aprons. It was spoken of as 'white sewing' as distinct from dress-making, which Lise was to take up. To begin with, Anne spent her working day standing at a table turning sewn straps of material right side out. She gave a demonstration of it at home, and imitated the people she worked with, until Selma was weeping with laughter. Anne thought pity akin to contempt and her pride demanded that she should be seen to be mistress of her own life.

She was not good with her hands. She had never made doll's clothes. (She had been given dolls as a matter of course but never played with them.) She could not draw. She pretended not even to know how to make a paper-chain. All activities which did not require much intelligence she assessed as beneath her. She took the job in the Katag because she did not have to ask for it: it was offered to her, Paul was able to do for her that much. She could not by whatever efforts have secured for herself something better.

She did not, to begin with, earn much, and that she kept, arguing that her parents ought not to benefit by her misfortune. Had they not expected to keep her at least until she had finished high school? Well then, that she was doing something else ought not to enter into their calculations. She was no longer asking them for money; that must make a difference which they ought not to overlook.

The firm was Jewish, though most of the management and the work-force were not. Anne assumed that here her Jewishness would not be a handicap and might even be an advantage. She stood over her inane job and as if she were Kate escaped into a story. One of the directors, or better still share-holders, someone young and unmarried, would come round and happen to see her and ask the manageress of the workroom, 'Who is that girl and what is *she* doing here?' She was not as pretty as Kate but she looked much more interesting; to the eyes of a worthy beholder she would be beautiful.

Quite unromantically, it was the manageress of the cutting room who noticed her and took her under her wing. 'For the sake of my conversation,' Anne said, not wanting to need to feel grateful; perhaps it was true. She said, 'As a trained cutter, I shall easily find a job somewhere abroad.' All she needed was time, and an aptitude for letting her ambitions lie fallow.

She was not, nor did she want to be reconciled. What was happening to her was unfair and, as she saw it, not to rebel against it was equivalent to agreeing with fate that she did not deserve better.

97

There was no place in her life for rebellion except in her head.

When Kate sometimes met her after work, Anne would tell her to wait at the corner of the street and not, most definitely not, outside the factory gates. Kate believed for many years that Anne was ashamed of acknowledging her as her little sister in front of the people she worked with, as when she was a schoolgirl she had not wanted her classmates to judge her by her sisters. This led Kate to believe that Anne valued the opinion of her fellow workers, that she valued them, that she valued her job – as Kate valued it and them for having become part of Anne's life. Only much later did she understand that Anne had not wanted to be seen by her as one of those workers coming out of that factory.

The prayer said by Jews after meals includes the Psalmist's observation that he had never seen the children of the righteous begging for food. This is always said silently so as not to risk offending anyone present. It used to offend Kate. For years it offended her so much that she failed to understand its meaning. Her family indeed did not need to beg for food or for any other charity on which they came to depend. It was freely given, to Selma and Paul in memory of her parents, and to their three daughters for Paul's and for Selma's sake.

For some months before Anne left school, she did not come straight home but went to eat her lunch in other people's houses. Dr Kronheim, the rabbi, arranged it or rather, he introduced the idea. He suggested to the family living next door to him that they should invite Anne to share a meal, and they enjoyed her visit so much that they asked her to come again, to come every Tuesday. Her hostess spoke of her to other still wealthy women, who also invited her – because they did not wish to be thought too poor or too mean, Anne said, salving her pride. It meant not only that Anne got better food and more of it, it also meant one mouth fewer to feed at home.

According to Jewish teaching, it is as much a good deed to accept charity as it is to dispense it: if there were no takers there could be no givers. Lise could not manage to see it like that when her turn came once Anne had started to work. To Anne it had been a challenge to enter the houses of those who saw themselves as socially her superiors and to establish her equality; Anne was always able to hold her own. Perhaps there was a little defensive malice in the imitations she gave of her experiences as a charity-eater. She understood – as some of her hosts apparently didn't – that it was not due to personal merit that they had so far been left more or less untouched by the Nazi laws. Lise felt herself to be so much less than people who lived in fine houses – finer by far than the one she had lived in even in Brackwede – that on the first occasion she went to the back door.

She could not eat and make polite conversation simultaneously. She believed that she was bound to be disappointing after Anne, and perhaps therefore she was: to get to know Lise you had to want to know her, and so only those who deserved her ever did. One hostess made her eat with the maid in the kitchen, and that was the only house she did not mind going to.

When the second family called off the arrangement, Dr Kronheim spoke about it to Selma. From a practical point of view, it made no difference which of her daughters ate charity. Perhaps people would be more willing to make allowances for Kate, if only because she was younger.

For Kate, the challenge lay in proving herself capable of doing what Anne had done; doing it less well she saw as letting Anne down. Pale and undersized as she was, with her big eyes and her greedy stomach, she was bound to make Jewish women want to feed her. She was less critical than Anne of what she ate and in whose company, and this must have increased her welcome. Word about her spread and before long she had so many invitations that so as to fit them all in, she went to some families only once a fortnight.

One of the households consisted of only father and son; they were both slaughtermen. Invariably, their housekeeper served goulash, with chunks of fat in it which made Kate, much to her embarrassment, gag when she chewed them and, when she swallowed them whole, brought tears to her eyes. Before the meal, she read to the old man from a newspaper; afterwards she fed the Great Dane chained in the yard, although she was terrified of it. It did not occur to her that she could have said no to something. There were worse things in her life: losing Ingrid's friendship, for instance. She saw it all as a part of being a Jew in Nazi Germany.

Another household consisted of only mother and son. Rosa Bonim and Selma had once been close friends. Selma's uncle Fishl had traded in model gowns, which had made Selma the best-dressed young Jewess in town; Rosa had worn her cast-offs.

Within walking distance of the Jahnplatz, Selma now lived like a recluse. It always surprised Kate to hear it when her mother said that she knew someone, but of course she knew people – she had been living in Bielefeld for most of her life. She and Rosa must have met accidentally, attending the synagogue on High Holy Days for instance, but they had not really spoken together for many years. More than once, Frau Bonim told Kate to bring her mother the next time. She would not come.

Perhaps she wanted to have nothing to do with her friends of former times because she was ashamed of her present state. Perhaps she had moved her family to the outskirts not only because rents were lower there but so as to discourage visitors. The only one who called on her repeatedly, about once a month, was the woman who peddled kosher margarine. Selma always invited her to sit down in the kitchen, which was also the living-room, and served her a cup of coffee using her best china.

Or perhaps the times had nothing to do with it. Before Hitler came to power, while living in Brackwede, Selma had had only minimal contact with people, though then the reason may also have been that she lived too far out. Perhaps she abjured having friends as she abjured piano-playing – which had certainly once been a source of great joy to her – because what she wanted out of life was not this sort of satisfaction but something else, which Kate when separated from her was too young to have understood.

In the later years in Kügler Street, Selma had a squared school exercise book for keeping her household accounts. To do this was her own idea: invariably, one of the first things she did after having been out of the house was to sit down at the kitchen table with this book and her purse and not leave off until she had accounted for every expenditure down to the last penny. She wrote very neatly, drawing her lines with a ruler or else making them wavy; such things as food and soap powder, for instance, went into separate columns. She had started the practice less to see where the money went than to find out where she might possibly make savings, but it became as important to her as if the bookkeeping itself were able to make what money Paul gave her go further.

Kate believed in her last years at home that her parents were on bad terms. At times her mother accused her father. Once, passing the doorway of a confectioner's, she paused and told Kate to take a good look at the blonde behind the counter: her father's taste was for that sort of floozie, henceforth referred to as 'the chocolate pig'. Once, walking with Kate into town, Selma stood still to indicate, there in the street, where her legs came up to beneath her clothing. She said, 'Your father likes his women with longer legs.' Was he ever unfaithful? Kate left home while she was at the stage when she would not have blamed him: what joy could ever have come to him from her fat sad mother?

Kate had never seen her naked, but in winter Selma liked to finish getting dressed by the kitchen stove, and the sight of her stuffing her flesh into her corset disgusted Kate. The dislike of her mother which Kate became aware of in adolescence was fuelled at least in part by jealousy: Selma had not only a prior, but a greater claim on Paul, since Kate could claim only a third of his fatherhood.

Selma liked to name things, personalizing her surroundings, scaling them down to manageable size. In Kügler Street, the vacuum cleaner – too old ever to work properly – became 'Hooverinchen', a name that feminized as well as diminished it. She had names for all the stoves before which she needed to go down on her knees, for the sharpest kitchen knife, for the floor-cloth. In later years, Paul, from being 'Paulchen', became 'The Consumer'. When her daughters demanded an explanation, she told them that she meant by this 'The Progenitor', only she did not like to make use of that word (presumably because of its sexual innuendo). (The German words *Erzeuger* and *Verbraucher* are more clearly opposites.) Kate, when she was old enough to think about it, suspected that the term expressed how she then felt about him.

Kate may well have altogether misinterpreted their relationship. Perhaps it was not her mother but Kate who held Paul responsible for what the Nazis were doing to the family and it was something she could not bear to admit even to herself?

Selma grew upset whenever Paul came home later than expected, which happened often. He was addicted to the company of men and would not have cut a conversation short because of the hour. The cause of Selma's anxiety at such times may not have been, as Kate believed, his philandering, but his reckless tongue: he would tell political jokes without caring who might overhear him. When she observed her mother weeping in his arms, this may not have been, as she believed, evidence of a reconciliation after a quarrel. Paul may have been trying to comfort her when she was in despair over their worsening circumstances.

Selma said of him that he had no culture and no taste. He did not read the classics, as she did; in fact he did not read books at all but only newspapers. He was not interested, as she was, in music. In the days when Jews had been allowed to enter such places, she had got him to take her to the theatre, the opera; his taste was more the music-hall, to which he went with his old comrades. He was not even much interested in visiting galleries and museums.

But professionally he was a man of standing. Among the houses he had designed was one faced with pale green ceramic tiles, some embossed, with a delicatessen on the ground floor, which still stands in one of the narrow streets of what was left by the war of the old town, and is now a listed building. Until Hitler came to power, he was on the roster of architects called upon by the local courts as experts. In the last competition he was allowed to enter, he submitted the winning design for the municipal savings bank. The building was put up in the name of the runner-up, an Aryan architect who was his lodge brother. It, too, is still standing.

Jews who were emigrating employed Paul to value their houses and to do the necessary paperwork. All he was commissioned to design in those days were tombstones, not only for the newly dead but also for the family graves being left behind by the emigrants, who paid generously. On leaving, they were obliged to hand most of their remaining money to the Nazis. Paul's style was affected by the changing times. The headstone he had designed for the grave of Selma's parents was of sandstone in the traditional ornamental style. Now he used a more durable stone and his lines were austere. The stones were instantly recognizable as his; they changed the character of a whole section of the cemetery.

When, towards the end of that year, a Jewish sculptor moved into the town, Selma blamed Dr Kronheim for befriending him: he would be taking work away from Paul. There were others who argued that the rabbi's first duty was to his own congregation. The congregation, with its ever-increasing responsibilities, was now in need of a book-keeper. And thus it came about that the job was given to Paul. It did not pay well and was only part-time, but it did for the next two years provide him with an income he could count on.

Indirectly, the appointment contributed to saving Lise's and Kate's lives. Before then, it helped to keep them clothed.

Every autumn, the community collected clothing for the needy, much of it was donated by shopkeepers and was therefore new. Their father arranged for Lise and Kate to go along and take their pick before the distribution. That was how, the following winter, they came to have their splendid new loden coats with hoods, Lise a green and Kate a reddish-brown one; they were so pleased to have them that they insisted on not taking anything else.

The only items never passed down within the family or accepted second-hand were shoes; this was where Selma drew the line and it caused problems. Because their feet were still growing they each had no more than two pairs, one on their feet and the other at the mender's. There was rarely money enough to collect more than one pair at a time – it was a question of whose soles were most badly worn. You put on the mended pair in the shop and left the other. Sometimes, when there was no money – unlike the corner grocer, the shoemaker did not give credit – both Lise and Kate wore the soles of their shoes right through. Once, on their way home in the rain, they stopped in a doorway for Lise to give her inlay soles to Kate, who had none and whose socks were worn through as well.

In the days before Anne started to earn, her shoes had priority, because the older a girl got the more her clothes mattered – or so she said, and the others accepted it. And collected her shoes for her because as a girl got older she couldn't be seen to be carrying a parcel. They did what they could for her; they did what they could for each other; their parents did for them what they could. In their family life they were fortunate and happy.

Ten

When, towards the end of the school year, the headmaster summoned Selma to tell her that Lise and Kate must also leave the Sarepta school, Kate at first believed (so ignorant had she remained of what was going on around her) that this was the consequence of Lise's non-attendance. This dates Selma's illness to the beginning of 1936.

Selma was fond of, was addicted to sleeping. She used to say that when she got up in the morning she looked forward to going to sleep after lunch and when she got up again she looked forward to going to sleep for the night. Therefore it did not surprise Kate, did not alarm her, when there came a time when she did not get up at all.

The only Aryan domestic help which Jews were still allowed to employ, if the household included a male over the age of sixteen, was a woman over the age of forty-five; like other Nazi laws it served the double purpose of being an advantage to Aryans while humiliating the Jews. Selma got eczema on her hands when she put them into cleaning water and also when she wore rubber gloves. So a woman still came twice a week for the rough work. Paid by the hour, she arrived late and left early, and Selma was grateful that she came at all. She was not someone to tend a sick Jewess.

Anne argued that she could not, so soon after starting at the Katag, ask for time off work, but this was understood to be merely an excuse: she could not have brought herself to be a servant to the others. Her share of doing what housework fell to the girls consisted of telling the other two that they were doing or had done it right. She made her own bed and dusted her part of the bedroom only because it was repugnant to her to have her belongings touched by anyone else. As far as Kate was concerned, Lise would have been willing to work through the night if this had been necessary to prevent her little sister's life from being disrupted.

While Selma had still been well enough to get up, Lise had helped her in addition to going to school. But she stayed at home to keep house for the family once Selma took to her bed, while she was in hospital, and for some days afterwards.

Lise was by nature more helpful than her sisters, and helping more at home in time resulted in her being better able to do so. She thought doing the chores a small price to pay for the approval it got her, for hearing the family say, 'Lise knows what to do' and, 'Lise knows how to do it'. She had long ago made the conscious decision to be good. Anne was praised for her brains and Kate for her looks. There was nothing Lise could do in these respects but she could do something about her behaviour. She did. She got praised for being unselfish and, craving more praise, she came to get emotional satisfaction out of being exploited – long before she felt a constant need to be punished for having broken her promise to their mother to look after Kate.

Selma had to have a tumour scraped from her womb. (Kate was to have a dead foetus scraped out at exactly the age her mother was then so perhaps Selma called it a tumour only out of delicacy.) Her stay in hospital was short enough to allow for only one visit.

It was still daylight when Lise and Kate set out from home on foot, to meet Anne coming from work; they waited for her as she had commanded them at the nearest street corner. Kate loved to be in town after the lights came on, especially on winter evenings when the cold made haloes about the street lamps, and especially when the rain made everything glisten.

'We shall walk,' Anne ruled, not because they were early, but so as to save the tram fare. This would allow her to buy, with the sum she was willing to spend (not all the money she had), grapes as well as a pineapple.

'You'll be the only one taking a present,' Kate pointed out, with the thought of borrowing money from her so as to buy something too. Anne waited until they had left the shop and she could not be overheard before explaining that Lise did not need to take anything:

her present to their mother was keeping house. Kate's present could be, if she wished, to carry the bag with the fruit.

As in every winter throughout her childhood Kate, though not her sisters, suffered from chilblains. Her fingers were swollen and red and itchy. They felt hot and the cold made them worse but she had not brought her gloves because they were so badly worn that Anne would have been ashamed to be seen with her wearing them. Lise lent her hers; their inside had the feel of Lise.

Anne always gave the impression of knowing the way to anywhere. If she went wrong she pretended that she had meant to make that detour in order to look at something. She always walked unhesitatingly; if she needed time to think she preferred to stand still. She always walked fast. Lise's legs were almost as long but Kate, to keep up, every now and again had to run a couple of steps.

Kate wanted to find their mother but she feared to arrive; doing anything for the first time was an ordeal to her. When the others were with her, Lise would tell her beforehand what to do and Anne would show her when the time came by example. But their presence was not always a blessing. Lise was sometimes an embarrassment and Anne often found fault.

They arrived at the gates of the hospital grounds and Kate wished that they hadn't, yet. 'Now remember,' Anne said as they walked up to the barracks-like building, every window alight. 'We're visiting Mutti for Mutti's sake, not our own.'

Outside the door beyond which their mother was lying, Anne called a halt and lined the three of them up, Indian file, in order of diminishing age and size. But thus she was unable to supervise the others. She must have found the occasion difficult, too: she stepped back and instead of issuing instructions, pulled Kate by the arm and pushed Lise back into place so that she had them standing in reverse order. She took her place at the rear and only then did she tell the nurse, who would have opened the door to the ward before if Anne had not told her to wait, 'Now we are ready.'

There were two beds in the room. Kate had not expected this, and for a brief moment regretted being first through the door, as if she were free to make a choice between the two women – the other being much younger and very pretty. But then, when she saw her mother, when she looked at her, she knew instantly that she would not have wanted to be anyone else's daughter, that this was the only possible, was the right mother for her. She felt that if she had been free to choose among a million women, this was the one she would have opted for, and if she had been told that she could not have her she would rather have gone without altogether than have anyone else.

Her mother smelled of hospital – or was it the bed? – and her flesh was warmer, but otherwise she was so totally familiar that Kate burst into tears – as the rivers run when the ice melts.

Anne removed the bag of fruit from where Kate had put it, on the bed. She tugged at Kate to make her get out of the way so that Lise and she could also greet their mother. As far as Kate was concerned, the rest of the visit was an anti-climax. It was a relief to her when it came to an end and not only because she urgently needed to pee.

On the way out of the hospital grounds – it had started to rain – passing some bushes not reached by the lights, she asked, 'Do you think anyone would notice me if I were to . . .?' Why had she not mentioned it before? Anne demanded to know. She could have gone to the lavatory inside the hospital. Kate had believed that these were meant only for the patients. Besides, there had been too many people about.

'We'll go on,' Anne said, taking Lise by the arm. 'If anyone says anything I shall say that we don't know you.'

When Lise and Kate had to leave the Sarepta school, Lise was three months short of her fourteenth birthday. Her marks at the end of that term were worse than ever, except in maths. The maths teacher was known to be difficult to please; he had a sharp tongue feared even by bright pupils. But he was also known to be fair, and Lise liked him. He called her out, one day, to solve a problem on the blackboard, explaining that he was testing her for a 'one' – rarely given by any teacher and not known ever to have been awarded by him. So overwhelmed was she by the occasion that she dropped the chalk and, having picked it up, stood there trembling and unable to think. One of her classmates began to laugh and soon all of them were laughing. Lise believed that the teacher had meant to make fun of her.

But, slinking past him back to her place, she heard him mutter, 'What a great pity.'

Among the Jewish schools then coming into existence was a boarding-school in southern Germany. Its headmaster was Hugo Rosenthal, from whom Selma had had her first proposal of marriage; his sister Alma had once been her best friend. Selma wrote to him, less in expectation of help than for advice.

He wrote back asking to see her daughters' school reports. Though the scholarships for the coming year had all been allocated, some would become available the following Easter. Selma saw no point in sending Lise's report – she sent Kate's, and Kate was offered a place. For the current year – while she was in the third form – she went to a secondary school for girls near the town centre, the Luisen school.

The change to a lesser school was good for her. The Sarepta school was élitist and clearly she did not belong with the élite. The girls in the Luisen school, being less privileged, were more tolerant. There were fewer flag-raising ceremonies; there was less enthusiasm for Hitler; what anti-Semitism there was fell to the lot of the only other Jew in the class, who had some of the faults ascribed to the Jews and made Kate, by comparison, seem almost as good as an Aryan.

'We don't mean you,' her classmates said on occasion. But Kate had learned better than to expect, let alone respond to, such friendship. She bought a picture postcard which looked just like a photograph of a teenaged girl; she glued it into her autograph book and, writing with her left hand, added a loving message. Thus she made the book fit for Luisen schoolgirls to write in.

They believed that she had come down in the world because she had not been bright enough for the grammar school. She did not realize this until, one day when she knew an answer which nobody else there knew, someone commented, 'Well, she's repeating the class, isn't she?' She tried to share her knowledge with them and not shame them – quite unlike the old, the younger Kate.

The memory of Herr Grote, her teacher of German there, was to remain with her. He reminded her of the violin-playing infant-school teacher, who in turn had reminded her of her Opa. He was important to her because of the kind of man he was, but also because of his subject: it was during her year with him that her knowledge of

German turned into an understanding of it, that she reached the stage of no longer taking the use of the language for granted, but began to make it serve her.

Lise was never to grow as tall as Anne. She grew taller than Kate, who stopped growing on leaving home. The best thing about Lise's appearance was her eyes of deep brown, but what made them beautiful was their sparkle, the goodwill towards the world that shone out of them. It wasn't Lise who was ugly – her character was too good – it was her emaciation and, what offended most in those days, her Jewish nose. Her chest was flat, her hips were as narrow as a boy's. Her thin arms and legs made her look – she was the first to say it – like a scarecrow.

Someone once asked her, when she was still fairly little, 'Why are you so thin?' and she answered, 'Because of the wind.' It became a family saying in response to any unanswerable question.

She once said to Selma, 'You love the others more than me just because they're nicer-looking.' It was not true – Lise herself did not believe it and she thought better of their mother than that. Kate did not feel more loved – she was just more frequently cuddled. Kate was jealous of Lise because of her goodness – as much beyond emulation as Anne's and her looks were for Lise.

Lise's readiness to help at home misled both her and Selma into believing that she liked doing housework, but she did have a passion for looking after younger children. There was a demand from Jewish women who could still afford it for what was called 'house-daughters': girls who would live as one of the family in exchange for doing a certain amount of work and receiving pocket-money. Lise herself and all who knew her believed that this would now be the best thing for her.

She became a house-daughter at the Blanks', who had a five-year-old daughter. They lived centrally, not far from the synagogue; in fact they lived next door to Tante Hete, in a street of large detached houses set in large gardens established enough to contain full-grown trees. Lise liked the idea of being able to go in and out of such a house as if she belonged there. Frau Blank employed a cook and a part-time cleaning woman. She wanted Lise chiefly, she told Selma, to be a big sister to Ruthie. It was agreed that she should get all her meals there, including breakfast, but continue to sleep at home. Lise went to be interviewed and believed herself lucky to have got the job.

Nothing about it was as she had been led to expect. Frau Blank was determined to give no one the right to call *her* a dirty Jew. She kept Lise dusting and polishing for hours,.which Lise minded chiefly because it was unnecessary – she almost preferred it when she had to do the rough work on the days when the cleaning woman did not come. Frau Blank supervised her closely and it grieved Lise not to be trusted. She ate in the kitchen and the cook served her the left-overs; the food was richer than she was used to and did not agree with her.

Ruthie was self-willed and tyrannical and Lise constantly feared not being able to control her. She had been forbidden to punish her and she was not supposed even to tell her off. 'I don't need to mind *you*,' Ruthie said. On evenings when the Blanks entertained, which they still did frequently, Lise remained to help with the washing-up and, finishing late, stayed the night. There was no bed for her except Ruthie's, who tried to keep it to herself all night long. And in the morning Frau Blank made Lise, since she was already there, start early to tidy and clean up after the night before.

Lise always tried to fulfil people's expectations of her; at the time she said nothing of all this at home. She grew thinner, and paler, and more nervous, and the change was put down to her age.

The Blanks' back door faced that of Tante Hete, who one morning happened to see Lise standing cleaning her master's shoes. She looked so much a waif that Tante Hete went straight to the telephone to ring Selma, and offered to pay Lise's school fees and something towards her keep for another year.

Lise then also went to the Luisen school. There she got good marks, surprising everybody including herself.

When Hitler came to power many people – not only Jews – believed that he would remain in office no longer than his predecessors. Paul believed it. He would have liked to believe that the discrimination against the Jews was not meant to affect people like him, who had for four years defended the fatherland on the Western Front and been awarded the Iron Cross, and came from a family which had been in

Germany for many generations. He thought of himself as a German citizen of the Jewish faith; as he did not believe in God this did not make him much of a Jew.

He was ten years older than the century. (Selma was three years younger than he.) Even in 1933, he thought of himself as too old to make a fresh start abroad when he was given the chance – it turned out to be the only chance to emigrate which he was ever to have. Max Heilbrunn, a business man preparing to move with his wife and children to Palestine, offered to take Paul and his family with him as his partner. Paul refused the offer for three reasons, the first of which was that Max Heilbrunn had once wanted to marry Selma – and Selma might have accepted him if Paul had not come along. Palestine was then thought of as a country for the young, or for the wealthy; with the whole world – in theory – to choose from, Paul would have preferred to go somewhere else. And if he could not again be an architect, he thought at that time, what was the point of transplanting himself and his family to another country?

It was Anne having to leave school that convinced him of the necessity to emigrate for the sake of his daughters. When the war broke out, he still did not believe that he and Selma would have benefited by becoming emigrants. Or that was how it seemed to Kate. She had the joy of looking forward of going to Herrlingen, Hugo Rosenthal's progressive boarding-school. She did not want the family to emigrate, unless this were to enable her to go to Ben Shemen, a children's village in Palestine – the term 'children's village' captivated her imagination. When Paul began to scan the advertisements in the *Jüdische Rundschau* (the only Jewish newspaper then still being published in Germany), to write letters, and to fill in forms, at first she hoped that nothing would come of it.

From 1935 onwards emigration was on the increase in Bielefeld; about half its Jews managed to escape abroad. It was possible to do so if you were wealthy; if you were in business and had at least some funds abroad; if you had relations abroad who were in a position to keep you or to employ you or to arrange for your employment; or if you had a trade or a profession which was, somewhere in the world, in demand. It helped if you were young; in every case it was essential to be healthy. There was something wrong with Paul's heart.

Nevertheless he endeavoured. There wasn't a country in the world which he did not at least think of taking his family to; there wasn't one accepting immigrants which he did not try, writing to embassies and architects and rabbis, to any office or person of whom he knew something which gave him reason, however minimal, for hope. Kate typed out the envelopes for him; she posted or went with him to post his letters. And instead of admiring him for his courage in continuing to try, she despised him as her mother did for his optimism, for wasting his time, for wasting money on stamps, when nothing ever came of anything. She was not old enough to know whether, all evidence to the contrary, he still expected one day to succeed, or whether he continued only because the alternative was to admit his defeat.

From the time that Lise and Kate had joined the Zionist movement, they lived with the possibility of emigrating without their parents, without Anne. Anne objected to Zionism on the grounds that one nationalism was as bad as another. Who your parents were, the colour of your skin, and where you were born, she argued, said nothing about your value as a human being, which depended solely on what you made of yourself. She did not wish to remain where she wasn't wanted, but to believe that as a Jew she could not live among non-Jews was too closely akin to Nazi thinking to be acceptable to her.

There was, when Anne was in her fifteenth year, the possibility for adolescent girls to emigrate to Australia; it was said that they were wanted for the marriage market. Kate imagined this as an actual place, something like the slave markets she had read about, where the girls would stand lined up, Anne among them, and young men, after looking them over, would take their pick. That Anne, who prided herself on being in charge of her life, should even consider such a thing brought home to Kate, more than all her father's efforts had done, how essential it was becoming for Jews to emigrate.

One Sunday morning, Anne told her to come for a walk; probably Lise was helping their mother in the kitchen but for ever after Kate chose to see the occasion as proof that she had been the preferred sister. They took the tram, Anne paying for both; unlike Lise and

Kate she did not enjoy walking. But on that occasion she wanted to climb up the hill to the castle and walk under the ancient beeches along the promenade, from where one could look down upon the town. Anne never did anything at random. She must have wanted to see that view to help her make up her mind.

Should she, or should she not, go to Australia? She was not, of course, asking Kate for advice; Kate understood this and kept silent. Anne wanted to argue the matter out with herself, and she needed Kate there so as to be able to do it aloud for greater clarity. If she had reached her decision before they returned home, she was keeping it to herself.

She would never have admitted that she was influenced by her sisters. It must have weighed with her that they were likely to go to the Land of Israel. Not putting her name down for Australia was Anne's first step towards Zionism.

It was at about this time that Paul began to design small pieces of furniture. It began with his invention of a footstool which was also a box for holding shoe-cleaning things; its lid could be propped up for the foot to rest on. He found a cabinet maker in the nearest village who was willing to go into partnership with him, an Aryan called Kindermann.

Before long they issued a glossy brochure with a choice of such things as occasional tables and wall-shelves. As Paul was the one who dealt with the customers, it was he who received the money – often he needed all of it too urgently to pass Kindermann's share on. The man would ring him up about it until Paul refused to answer the telephone; he made his daughters answer it and if it was Kindermann tell him that he was out. That was the sort of thing the Nazis did to the Jews which is not mentioned in the history books: they made upright men tell their children to tell lies.

Paul's financial problems were compounded by the practice of settling debts with bills of exchange: these were passed on and when they fell due, if the debtor did not pay Paul, Paul could not pay his creditor, and whoever was then in possession of the bill would sue the Jew in the chain of signatories. Then the bailiffs would come and affix a sticker – it bore the German eagle and was for some reason referred to as 'the cuckoo' – usually to the back of the piano and sometimes to the back of the couch as well. These items could not then be sold by the owners and, if the debt was not settled within seven days, would be confiscated and auctioned.

That her father always managed somehow or other to avert this catastrophe, made Kate continue to have a childish faith in his powers.

Eleven

The *Stürmer* was displayed behind glass in cases put up in the streets and especially at tram stops, where people while waiting had nothing better to do than to look at or even read it; Lise and Kate found it impossible to ignore. The lead stories were always about sex and violence: Jewish men doing unimaginable things to Aryan virgins; other articles were about Machiavellian politics and financial swindles perpetrated by 'international Jewry'. The line-drawings caricaturing the Jews were never so extreme that one could not recognize one feature here, another there, as those of people in the community.

Of course Lise and Kate did not believe what they read. But they did not totally disbelieve it either, and the memory of what they had read remained.

At school, they were excused from attending the lessons in religion; Kate liked to sit through them, and listened although pretending to read. At least once – in the Luisen school – when no one responded to a question, she could not resist the temptation of putting her hand up; the answer she gave was right. In that school there was no morning assembly; in the Sarepta school, the three Jewish girls had been obliged to be present but were not expected to take part. The Nazi rituals and ceremonies were much more of a problem: to ask permission to stay away from them or to attend but not participate both drew equal attention to their otherness, which Kate especially found hard to bear. Unlike Anne, she was incapable of believing that it was everybody else who was wrong.

She found it impossible not to believe that there was at least some truth in what the Nazis were saying about the Jews, who were being accused by them so comprehensively that even a little of it amounted to quite a lot. There must be something the matter with the Jews: the

Nazis were not the first anti-Semites, they were not the only ones. The Jews had always, everywhere, sooner or later, been persecuted, and what was the single common factor in all these instances except the Jews?

The Zionists claimed to know the answer but, being Jews themselves – and were Jews not liars and cheats? – probably ought not to have been believed. Of course they would argue – it was only to be expected of them to make excuses – that it was not the nature of the Jews but their position in society by which anti-Semitism was provoked. 'Give us a homeland,' the Zionists said, 'and we shall prove ourselves to be like everyone else.' Anne argued that then the advantages of being a Jew would disappear together with the disadvantages. Kate could not see what the advantages were – or if she did, she did not value them much. To be like everyone else was what she wanted; she was willing to go to Palestine to achieve it. Besides, to leave Germany for any other destination was futile: you, or your children, or your children's children would one day have to suffer the same experience all over again.

Anne said, 'I would be against the Nazis even if they suddenly started loving the Jews.' When Kate grew old enough to understand why she said this, she agreed. But not wanting to be a Nazi was different from wanting to be a Jew.

Kate thought it was preferable to be a Christian because Christianity had grown out of Judaism. She believed in human progress, so what came later in time must therefore be better. Also, she valued herself so little that she believed anything *she* could have not worth having. (Which may explain why she valued Lise less than Anne, her mother less than her father – however much she clung emotionally to Selma and Lise.) It was being left no choice about it that made being a Jew like living with a halter round one's neck.

There were in Bielefeld a few orthodox Jews, mostly of Polish origin; between them and assimilated families like the Loewenthals there was little common ground. The orphans in Rüdesheim had been the first orthodox children Kate had had anything to do with, and she had envied them their certainties. Envy being with her a driving force, this had started her off in the direction of orthodox Judaism. But it was not until she arrived in England stripped of everything German that she said to herself, if I've got to be Jewish then I shall be that in every possible way and as much as I possibly can.

Then she became truly orthodox for a couple of years or so – until she began to find an inner stability. The first to teach her some of the knowledge of Judaism which she needed then was not Friedemann but Dr Kronheim.

She could not profit from being taught by Friedemann: during his lessons her emotions, so to speak, wrapped themselves round her brain. She learned the rudiments of the Hebrew language and of Jewish history not because of but in spite of him. In the spring of her thirteenth year, Anne, Lise, Kate and two other girls were, together, prepared by Dr Kronheim for their bat-mitzvah – a confirmation ceremony for girls which liberal Judaism copies from Christianity. It is normally held, if at all, when a girl is twelve; Anne and Lise had been made to wait until Kate was old enough, because Selma wanted it so.

The five girls, dressed in white, stood on the dais in the synagogue, in a semicircle facing the congregation, and in turn recited a chosen text. Lise and Kate, doing this, as well, together, had chosen the 121st Psalm from, 'I will lift up mine eyes unto the hills . . .' to '. . . he that keepeth Israel shall neither slumber nor sleep.' Lise recited the words in German after Kate, who was first because she was the youngest, had recited them in Hebrew. Never before had this congregation heard the language spoken by a girl and it responded as trees do to a gust of wind. Anne, being the eldest, came last; she had chosen the passage in which a boy asks an old man, 'How did you come by your wisdom?' and he answers, 'By never being ashamed to ask a question.'

It was Pentecost, and the synagogue had been decorated with greenery as never before. It may even have been the first bat-mitzvah to take place there. The persecuted Jews were finding their way back to God, albeit in an assimilated manner.

Anne had been saving up for a holiday. She had made the decision to have one and had chosen where to go – to a place on the Baltic coast not far from where, as a child, she had walked in protest into the sea.

She had booked a room in a boarding-house and paid a deposit – all despite a certain amount of opposition from her parents, who thought that she was too young to go on holiday alone and also that she ought not to spend all the money she earned on herself.

One afternoon, when Kate came into her parents' bedroom, her mother, still in her underwear, drew her attention to how shabby it was and said, 'It isn't right that Anne has such fine things and I have only these; it never occurs to her to buy something for me.' She made a similar comment when Anne bought herself a large beige handbag; hers was of lacquered black leather, criss-crossed with cracks and with the corners worn into holes. She tended to dwell on her grievances with Lise and Kate, but she had learned not to nag Anne.

When Kate – seldom if ever Lise – did something to displease her, if she saw the offence as serious enough it would prompt her to say, 'The best years of my life I have sacrificed for you girls.' Anne called this moral blackmail. Kate might say on occasion that she hadn't asked to be born, but only Anne dared to act as if they did not owe their parents anything.

That summer the Katag was Aryanized and all the Jewish employees lost their jobs. When Anne announced this at home, the first thing Selma said to her was, 'Don't worry, you shall have your holiday. Papa will find what money you still need.' It was a catastrophe, what had happened to Anne. By now no Jew could find another job like it. And she had nothing to show – no piece of paper to further her chances of emigration – for the seven or eight months she had spent in the Katag.

That the loss of such a job should be considered catastrophic by a girl like Anne was in itself a catastrophe.

Nobody in the family dared to say 'Poor Anne' to her face. But she must have known – and hated – that that was what they were thinking; they betrayed it. Paul handed her more money than she had asked for. Selma made her a new dress, out of a large fringed silk shawl she owned, beige with an abstract pattern hand-painted in bold colours; it had lain folded away but Selma cherished it. Lise and Kate looked for things they could do for Anne.

Poor Anne, reduced to being comforted by such favours.

Also that summer, the Jewish Women's Association included Lise among the children to be sent away. The doctor recommended sea air and she went to Norderney, an island just off the coast in the North Sea. She came back after a fortnight, still white-faced and all bones. She must have told Selma all about it, she must have written letters home. Kate could not bear to have anything to do with that part of Lise's life in which she had no share. All the other children had been younger and the staff had made use of her as another helper, which Lise had enjoyed being – at the expense of her health.

Kate needed to have a best friend to help her free herself from her dependence on Lise. Earlier that year she had found one in a Jewish girl called Helga. Black-haired, brown-eyed and skinny, physically she resembled Lise; like Anne she was the eldest. She was a year younger than Kate, who saw herself as dominant in the relationship.

It was Kate's idea that Helga should come with her to Rüdesheim. The Jewish Women's Association agreed to send them both. 'Wasn't it nice of Papa to arrange it?' Kate commented to her mother, who told her, 'He didn't do it for you, he did it for Erna Schwarz.' Helga's mother, separated from her husband, was tall and slender and always very well dressed, her hair professionally set, her hands manicured, her face made up. Kate, reaching puberty, though still totally baffled by the subject of sex, could see why Paul might prefer her to Selma. But as a mother she was too selfish and lacking in warmth. Compassion, more than any other emotion, was what prompted Kate to feel love. She loved Helga not only for herself but for having such a mother, for having a missing father, for not having Anne and Lise but only a little sister.

Not only had Helga never before been away from home, but Kate had already been where they were going. Kate foresaw herself looking after Helga.

Again, the other children in the home had all come together from Cologne, but this time from a different orphanage. They were older, included boys in their teens, and were not at all orthodox. They jeered at Kate for expecting them to say grace, for saying it, and for refraining on the Sabbath, for instance, from making a daisy-chain.

Kate was so made that she took a compliment received by another in her hearing as a criticism of herself. That Anne was frequently commented on as bright made Kate believe against all the evidence that she herself was stupid; because Lise was thinner and her thinness more talked about, Kate believed that she herself was fat – a misapprehension reinforced by the generally held opinion that there was a striking physical resemblance between her and her mother.

Perhaps to begin with the other children did not like Helga better than they liked Kate; they would not have prejudged them. But Helga was more outgoing. A half-smile from another was enough to make her smile back, whereas Kate would wait for a second smile to make sure that she had not been mistaken – especially if it came from someone with whom she wished to make friends. The more popular Helga became, the more Kate's pride forbade her to compete with her. Every 'Helga, Helga!' she heard as a 'Not you, Kate.'

One day as they were coming into the dormitory for their afternoon rest, Kate, finding herself by chance alone with Helga, blurted out, 'I brought you here, you ought not to gang up with the others against me.' Helga argued that she was not doing that, that having come there together was no reason for not making other friends, that – this in answer to Kate's response – she would make friends with whomsoever she chose.

By this time they were no longer alone. 'You tell her!' one of her new friends encouraged Helga.

Kate's arguments, meant to move Helga, moved only herself; she could not go on talking for fear of beginning to cry. She reached out and pulled Helga's hair. Within moments, they were grappling on the floor, scratching and biting. The spectators sided with Helga – slighter-looking but stronger – and cheered her on. Kate, needing to choose between hurting and being hurt, wanted neither: only boys fought like this, and she knew what her mother thought of such boys. She was appalled to have got into a fight and would have been ashamed of being capable of winning it. Also, she knew that it would not have got her what she wanted. Yet to have yielded was not in her nature.

Some member of staff, drawn by the noise, arrived and put a stop to the fight. She made Kate and Helga shake hands. They avoided looking at each other while doing so and remained unreconciled.

Helga gathered up her belongings from the bed beside Kate's while sundry girls clamoured for her to become their neighbour.

This time, Kate thought, not even a real attack of appendicitis could save her. When they got back to Bielefeld, everybody would hear of what had happened. That Helga would not want this either did not occur to her.

In the days when Kate and Lise had met with the neighbourhood children under the balcony, a boy had once crawled out, walked a few steps, and relieved himself against the wall under Anne's window. Kate, looking after him to see what he was getting up to, had caught a side view of his penis. She had never seen her father naked. Lise had shown her the illustrations in his encyclopaedia, but these were not explicit enough to teach Kate anything, and Lise did not think herself competent to explain them. In the children's home, the summer of her thirteenth birthday, Kate became for the first time attentive to the bulge in boys' trousers.

There were eight lavatories, four on either side of the passage that led to the showers. All were for the use of both boys and girls. The lavatories had no fastenings on the doors, which did not quite reach the ground, so that it could be seen whether or not a stall was occupied: the feet showed. The doors had swing hinges and some-times boys punched them so that, rebounding, they would swing open for a glimpse of a squatting girl. Kate believed that it was the girl who was thereby shamed; she feared it happening to herself.

The partitions were of cheap wood, painted forest green. 'Have you noticed anything about them?' some girl one day asked her and she answered that she had: they gave you splinters. 'The knot-holes, silly,' her informant told her. The left-hand end stall had one through which you could observe the boys in the showers. 'Then they can see us!' Kate exclaimed, aghast. They couldn't, it was explained to her: the girls, when it was their turn to shower, made sure that the stall was occupied by one of them. But the boys did not mind being looked at; some even enjoyed it and showed themselves off.

Kate joined in the spying on the boys more because she felt flattered to be counted among the big girls than because she wanted to see. Anne had drawn her attention to the contradiction inherent in thinking nakedness shameful while believing that man was made in God's image. Anne doubted the existence of God and did not show herself naked. Perhaps seeing boys was tantamount to looking at God? Kate wondered. The previous year, she would have looked unhesitatingly, with the unselfconscious curiosity of a child; she did not, like Lise, refrain from doing anything she could not have told their mother. But she did not want to break one of the commandments.

And so she squatted for a token look: sufficient not to be dismissed by the other girls as too little and laughed at, not enough to indulge her God-given sinful senses. What she saw was bouncing cocks and balls – she could not see the faces of the boys these belonged to. As far as she was concerned, the anonymity of the parts deprived the sight of them of all its effectiveness.

Her fight with Helga had left her unwilling to look people in the eye; she was just beginning to get over this when spying through the knot-hole left her again too embarrassed.

There was a boy, Ludwig, whom she had been noticing. He was big for his age, and at first she had thought him older. He was too big for his clothes, it gave him an oafish look. But he had dreamy blue eyes, at variance with his wide, ready grin. His brown hair was curly and his ears stood away from his head. Once, on a walk through the forest, he had sought her out, but only so as to ask a question so inane that she had preferred instantly to forget it. What she remembered was how she had felt, seeing him coming towards her – as if her lukewarm heart had suddenly boiled over.

She preferred to believe that he had not been among the boys whom she had seen in the showers.

She was still afraid of the dark or rather, between nightfall and dawn she was afraid even indoors with the lights on. At home, she made Lise come with her then to the lavatory; before getting into bed she made Lise look under it. No one looked under the beds in Rüdesheim.

One evening after lights out, she felt something touching her mattress from below; immediately afterwards there were exclamations and giggles, not only those of girls. Pandemonium broke out and then the light was switched on: half a dozen boys came out of their hiding-places. The boy who had been under Kate's bed was Ludwig.

This so amazed her that she told herself that it didn't mean anything, he had probably not known whose bed it was. If the purpose had been, as some girls said, to watch them undress, and he did know which bed was whose, then he was interested in somebody opposite her, diagonally opposite, probably Helga. Speculation was turned into certainty by self-contempt. Nobody else, not her mother, not Lise, knew all she knew about herself and therefore, none of the love she received could reassure her.

It was rumoured that the exploit had been Ludwig's idea. She didn't care. No one, nothing, could have got her to admit that she was, that she had been, interested in him. Establishing a relationship made you vulnerable, as her friendship with Ingrid, her friendship with Helga had taught her. From now on her loving was something she would do secretly and by herself.

Twelve

That autumn, one of the local cinemas showed *The Pied Piper of Hamelin*. A special afternoon performance was put on for school-children. In Kate's class, those who wanted to go to it were told to put up their hands; Kate did and was also counted. 'It won't be up to the school,' they told her at home. 'Don't be disappointed if they won't let you in.'

That, throughout the performance, she was feeling uncomfortable had nothing to do with the film or with the Nazis. She thought she must have eaten something that had disagreed with her. She had walked to the cinema, and she walked home from it as dusk was falling and the lights were coming on – her favourite time for being out in the streets.

When she got back, her mother was standing ironing in the kitchen. To entertain her, Kate impersonated the Pied Piper, playing her recorder and prancing about, in high spirits – the sort of high spirits her mother always warned her would end in tears. It had been a double treat, to go to the cinema at all and to go together with her classmates. It did not suffice to explain her euphoria. She still had those nagging abdominal pains but moving about seemed to ease them.

It felt to her as if prancing and laughing were causing her bladder to leak. She put her hand into her pants and it came away bloody.

'Look, Mutti!' she shouted as if, still, nothing were true for her until it was shared with her mother. 'I have the curse, tra-la-la,' she sang, pleased beyond measure at this proof that at last, in this respect at least, she had caught up with her sisters.

Anne may still have intended to become a lawyer, but she no longer talked about it. What she now said about her future was that she would marry an English lord. Kate was used to Anne doing what Anne said she would, and believed that she meant it. With Kate, fantasies were an escape from reality but with Anne they were rehearsals for intentions. She now sought a job as a house-daughter in a spa, to give herself the chance of meeting some eligible young Englishman – or just anybody from abroad who would help her to emigrate: a future employer, perhaps. She must have hoped for some such alternative to getting married.

Bad Oeynhausen was not much farther than Bad Salzuflen. But to save money she did not go for an interview; everything was arranged by letter. After a fortnight, she came home for a Sunday, in one of her talkative moods. She not only talked about her employers but impersonated them. Her mistress searching through the larder for something to give Anne for breakfast: some left-overs which the dog would not want to eat. Her mistress standing by while Anne sorted the washing – Anne would have to wash her master's dirty under-pants by hand, because of what people would think of the household if they were sent to the laundry.

Her family laughed with Anne. It was what she wanted of them, not for them to feel sorry for her. She was good at making them laugh; she could make Selma laugh even when she felt more like crying and, anticipating what Selma would say – which she was also good at – she would imitate her. 'It isn't a laughing matter, I'm laughing only because of my raw nerves.'

It would not be true to say that Kate idolized Anne. That would imply that her opinion of Anne was higher than she deserved. What is one to think of this fifteen-year-old who, until then refusing even to help dry the dishes, was now making a joke of being exploited by strangers? But what else could she have done to preserve her regal pride?

Seven years later, in a Bristol hospital, before the operation which she survived for no more than six days – by which time everyone was hopeful that she had been cured – Anne made the people looking after her laugh, with her jokes about her condition, while she made up her mind whether or not to agree to the experimental removal of her spleen, knowing that if this did not restore to her blood its ability to clot, it would result in her death.

After six weeks in Bad Oeynhausen, Anne returned home.

Selma was, perhaps, always over-anxious about her daughters' health. She took Kate to the doctor much more frequently than Kate was in need of treatment. There was not, then, anything seriously wrong with Anne. She had always been irritable. The nerve specialist to whom Selma took her prescribed bromide. A tin of this joined Kate's packet of glucose, which stood on the kitchen shelf; but Anne felt justified in her response to the world and rebelled against being sedated.

She had learned French at school; she thought that it would be useful to her to know English also. Paul and Selma agreed to let her enrol for a six-month course.

In the seventeen and a half years of his active fatherhood, Paul resorted to physical violence only twice. One afternoon when they were still living in Brackwede, Selma was sleeping upstairs – she felt unwell. Paul had got up and was in the next room, Anne and Kate were quarrelling. They often did; it was for Kate one of the ways in which she related to Anne, made herself matter to her. Anne could drive her wild by a word or a look, or by ignoring her. And then Kate would shout. Making up in volume for what she lacked in size, Anne called it.

Lise was telling them to be quiet and it was her voice Paul heard as he came into the room. He took hold of her and slapped her bottom once, hard. She knew that she had not deserved this and therefore did not let it upset her.

The second occasion was on a winter afternoon when Anne was studying English. Jews were no longer allowed in public places of entertainment, but in Bielefeld you could still risk going to the cinema. Most people there did not, individually, manifest hostility – unless it happened to be to their advantage: a neighbour might denounce a Jew because he coveted his house or flat. Children, especially if they were in uniform, would curse Jewish children and throw stones. When it happened, you turned back to go by another route or waited until they had gone. To stand your ground or even retaliate could only make matters worse for a Jew. There were group attacks, like the one in which Friedemann among others was injured;

they were rarely spontaneous and passers-by might stop to watch but were unlikely to join in.

Going to the cinema was a rare treat, less because it was forbidden than because it cost money. One day Anne got ready to go and then discovered that her parents were also going. She went past Lise and Kate back behind the curtain and took her coat off again. Paul followed her. It had long been accepted within the family that Anne preferred to do things by herself; it must have been something she said, or the way she said it, that had upset him. He pushed her on to her bed, turned her over, and with his flat hand slapped her bottom, again and again and again. And nobody stopped him, they were all too aghast.

This was also the winter in which Paul bought a lightweight motor bicycle. He had not ridden either a horse or a bicycle since his youth; he was a heavy man and middle-aged. But he wanted to go further afield in his search for work on the margins of architecture, and as a middleman. If he was a failure, he was at least a trier.

He employed Kate to help him learn the highway code and he paid her for it. He was not mean with money when he had it; when it came to him unexpectedly he would give his daughters each a small sum, unasked. There would be a twinkle in his eyes as he told them to 'save it against a rainy day' – because of his habit of borrowing it back, as he did the money that he gave them on such occasions as birthdays and Hanukkah, if he happened to have some just then. If not, and when he borrowed from them, he solemnly issued IOUs, which always remained unredeemed. On the other hand, if they had in the meantime spent the money he had told them to save for him, nothing more was said about it.

Soon after the move to Kügler Street, he began to deal in something packaged in small flat boxes, glossy white with red lettering and the head of a woman in silhouette. They arrived stacked flat, still needing to be folded. Only later did Kate understand that they were used to supply condoms by post. When that business failed they were burned. But the stationery printed for his other ventures – a building society, an insurance agency – she was allowed to have when no longer wanted; she trimmed off the letterheads on her father's guillotine and stitched the blank sheets into notebooks and pads. She developed such a passion for these that she could not get enough of them. One Friday afternoon she took some stationery which she knew was still in use – and forgot everything on the table when called to get ready to go to the synagogue.

On their Sunday family walks, Selma liked to play a game: she would let their daughters walk ahead and then say to Paul, in a voice loud enough for them to hear, 'What nice girls those are, do you think they will mind if we speak to them? Do you think we might ask them to come home with us?' and other such nonsense. The game probably stemmed from her endeavour, one day, to make up with them after a quarrel.

That Friday afternoon, the three were walking ahead when Selma called to Kate. The others also stopped but Selma told them to go on; it was Kate she and Paul wished to speak to. Taking what did not belong to you was stealing, they pointed out; having stationery printed cost money which they could ill afford. Next time she wanted some paper, would she please ask for it?

Their gentle chiding was harder to bear than punishment would have been.

In the days when Adolf Schönfeld had been its president, the Jewish community had always held a children's Hanukkah party. One of Kate's earliest memories is of her grandfather coming into the hall with a multicoloured bunch of gas-filled balloons to distribute; she tugs at his arm for attention, he lets go, and they all rise up to the ceiling. It was a family tradition that for the occasion the sisters received new dresses, a little too big so that they would do for best throughout the coming summer; they were blindfolded when they tried them on because they counted as presents.

It was a sign of the times when, instead, the young Zionists put on an entertainment for the adults. In 1934 their play required a small girl; they came to ask Selma for Kate, to whom play-acting was abhorrent. They made do with Lise instead. The role was that of a self-sacrificing child of poverty-stricken parents, and it suited her so well that Selma was overwhelmed with congratulations for her daughter's acting ability.

Afterwards, some young Nazis lying in wait challenged some of the young Jewish men to a fight. Among those who were hurt – none of them badly – was Friedemann. From then on, after blessing the congregation at the end of every synagogue service, Dr Kronheim said, 'Disperse quickly, go home in twos and threes and avoid attracting attention.'

The following year, no communal Hanukkah celebration took place: the local Zionists had lost their most active leaders through emigration. In 1936, therefore, the organization sent a young man from Cologne.

His nickname, Baby – because he had a pronounced lisp – preceded him. No one in Bielefeld knew anything else about him. But there was among the Zionist children much excitement about his imminent arrival, especially among the girls who were old enough to be interested in boys just because they were boys. Lise and Kate were still at the stage of despising them for it. (Not long before, the girl who led their group had taken Kate aside to ask her what was the matter with Lise, that she was not yet interested in boys? Perhaps she was, but was too shy, too unsure of herself to show it and thought Kate too young to be told, or perhaps she was holding herself back so that Kate could keep up with her.)

Baby had a shock of black hair standing on end, and very deep-set, very dark brown eyes. He was young for his task but the nickname was misleading. 'You will kindly address me as Bernt,' he told them. His face was austere and he took himself seriously.

Kate remained in the children's synagogue choir for Friedemann's sake, someone beside Lise whom he could count on to be well behaved – she had grown out of being pleased with her singing. She refused to be in the Hanukkah choir. She refused to be cast for the play. 'If you don't want to contribute you don't need to come to rehearsals,' Bernt said. She had hoped to escape his notice – he aroused in her feelings with which she could not cope. She did want to contribute, and not only so as to justify her continuing presence at rehearsals; she was by now a convinced Zionist and a bit of a propagandist.

Thinking about their programme on her way home that day, she thought that something was lacking, it was not explicit enough. What there was could be dismissed as no more than childish entertainment by people like her father – and there were many – whose Jewishness would have made no difference to their lives if it had not been for the Nazis.

As soon as she got home, she went to the bedroom where she could be by herself. Standing at her bedside table, in light subdued by the curtain which had been left closed by Anne, she made her first poem. Writing in pencil on scrap paper, she put the words down, one, two, or a line at a time, once she had considered them and recognized them as right. She was not inventing, the words were there within her mind; all she needed to do was wait until they came forward. It was not much different from her mother making a shopping-list.

The poem began, 'Wake up, Jews!' and went on to say that they ought not to leave it to others to decide what their Jewishness meant, that they should learn to see it as an asset instead of as a burden, that they should decide to emigrate to the Land of Israel not because they were no longer wanted in Germany but because that was where they should want to be.

She copied it on to clean paper in her best writing and took it with her to the next rehearsal. During unorganized moments Bernt was constantly besieged by people. She did not want to compete with the others for his attention; she wanted it not for herself but for her poem. And she wanted her poem to be taken seriously, which she believed would not happen if he knew that it came from that despicable Kate. Over anything else she would have enlisted Lise's help, but Lise did not even know about the poem. Going away on holiday was an act of no more than physical independence; it was making a poem that was Kate's first truly autonomous act.

She hung about near Bernt until he asked her, 'Have you got something to say to me?' He was being patronizing rather than kind. Her mother had told her often enough, liar that Kate was, that no good ever came of lies. Without a word, she offered him her poem. He read it, and read it again before asking her where she had got it. He as good as prompted her to say, 'I found it in a book.'

'That was lucky,' he said. 'Do you understand what it means? If you do, would you like to recite it?' It would make an excellent prologue.

A stage with a curtain had been put up in that part of the hall which was usually shut away behind folding doors and used as an office. Chairs had been set out until there was almost no gangway and they were all filled. A hush fell when most of the lights were switched off. Bernt, standing in the wings, beckoned Kate to him. 'Nervous?' he whispered, and she wished that he hadn't. It wasn't the right word for what she was feeling; she shook her head.

He smiled at her but she did not smile back – her face was already composed for when the curtain would open. Briefly the young man laid his hand on her head.

And suddenly she understood what it was she was feeling for him; it was what explained everything Anne had always said she was too young to understand. Anne was sitting out there somewhere in the audience, with their parents. Lise or Kate would have sat between them, but Anne would be sitting to one side, or even a seat or two away as if she did not belong with them. The impression she would be making on Anne was what Kate thought of as Bernt stepped in front of the curtain to greet the audience and to announce her. The discovery which she had just made – that she was in love with him – would have to wait. First, her poem.

There can have been few people in the hall who, even if they had never before thought about Kate, did not know her as one of Adolf Schönfeld's granddaughters; did not recognize her, either by her resemblance to her mother or because they had seen her about with her father, and everybody knew Paul Loewenthal. She must have looked very small, very solitary, up there on the big, otherwise empty stage. Very pale, having refused all make-up. Very serious, with her heavy eyebrows.

That voice which could not keep a tune could sing with words. The hall was large enough to seat several hundred people and there was no microphone. But Kate's every word could be heard distinctly in the furthest corner. It must have startled people, that that slight child had such a powerful delivery.

The spectacle of her was what made her poem so effective. Or so everybody except Anne said afterwards, when it became known that she had made it up. Anne said, 'They don't want to admit having been moved by the words of a child.'

Cultural evenings had begun to be held in the synagogue itself. The following month, the programme consisted of music for piano and violin, and a recital of her own poems by Hilde Marx, from Berlin. Now that Jews were no longer allowed to appear except before Jewish audiences, the performers were sometimes world-famous. Kate did not know whether or not Hilde Marx was famous; she could not afterwards say whether or not she had liked her poems: she had not been able to hear them because all her senses had been responding to the occasion.

Afterwards, people who knew Kate, including some whom Kate did not know, said to her, 'One day you will be standing there like that reciting your poems.'

She did not make poems because she wanted to be famous. If she did want to be famous it was only because that would have been good for her poems. It was her poems she wanted to have known, not herself. What the occasion did for her was to make her realize that poetry could be made to matter as much as music – that paradise for ever beyond her reach. For a short time that evening at least, Hilde Marx had been treated as if she were the equal of Mozart. It reconciled Kate to the kind of talent she had, though as with everything else she would have liked more of it.

She saw herself as serving it. Rilke wrote that if you can live without making poems then you are not entitled to make them. By the time Kate read this a few years later in his *Letters to a Young Poet*, she had already discovered for herself that to make a poem, wanting to make one simply wasn't enough.

What was needed was a willingness, a readiness. And if you were lucky a poem would come to you as the weather comes from the horizon. First you would recognize what it was to be about and then it would make its shape known to you as a melody. Then you had to keep all thought at bay – whatever you were doing, you could not think about that or anything else but only about your poem – about that you needed to think, but without words. It was having this ability to think without words that enabled Kate to make poems.

She made them in her head, mostly while she was by herself and walking. The words would come into her mind like doves to their cote. She did not write anything down until it was as good as she could make it. Writing words down gave them independence and only then could she judge them; but if she then found them to be not right there was no longer anything to be done about it.

She did not make many poems. She made them all, like her first one, about the Jewish condition. Until she left home that was for her the only theme with enough pressure behind it to flush them out.

She learned not to show them to her mother, whose way of encouraging her was to suggest what she saw as improvements, which caused dissension between them. Her mother believed that as an adult she knew better, while Kate believed that she knew better because it was her poem. She did not show them to her father because she did not think him sufficiently literate. She did not show them to Anne because it would have degraded them to be used to get her Anne's praise. She learned not to show them even to Lise after Lise had praised what afterwards she herself came to find wanting. Lise approved too indiscriminately of whatever she did, and her poems deserved better.

Instead, she sent them to the *Jüdische Rundschau*; the editor of the children's supplement usually accepted them. Once she sent him a poem for Shavuot (Pentecost); it arrived too late and was held over until the following year, when it appeared giving her age as a year younger than she was by then. People commented on it, and it vexed her to have to explain what had happened until Anne said, 'That was the greatest compliment the editor could have paid you.'

Before long, he paid her a greater. He wrote to her that if it had not been for her age, he would be printing her poems in the main part of the paper: they were mature enough.

This was because they always said more than she had known she knew.

Thirteen

The journey between Bielefeld and Herrlingen took seven hours, plus the waiting times for connections in Cologne and Ulm. Kate would have welcomed travelling even further. She wanted to get out of her life and into another, and was still naïve enough to believe that this could be done by getting away from home.

It was always easy for her to part from her family – what she found difficult was being away from it. At the root of her constitutional impatience was her anxiety that she would not be able to cope. Hers was the Till Eulenspiegel temperament, which rejoices in adversity when things can only get better and grieves at good fortune because now they are bound to get worse. For much of the time, she concerned herself not with life but with some story going on in her head.

After changing in Cologne, she knew that there were other children on the train travelling to the same boarding-school. She made no attempt to find them. Instead, she fantasized being found by a somewhat older boy with curly hair and dark eyes. There must have been someone like that in her past, perhaps Günther the magpie-tamer, because it was not beauty she was after but a likeness: he had ears like pot-handles and a wide-mouthed grin. Ludwig, in Rüdesheim, had come close.

With some of the most spectacular reaches of the Rhine before her eyes, and the most drastic change yet in her life only hours ahead, she was cocooned from reality inside her day-dream. 'Do you know which is the Lorelei Rock?' she would ask. 'Have you read much Heine?' and either he would have read everything she had or nothing at all. He would be her mirror-image or her complement; she could not make up her mind which she would prefer.

On the windy station in Ulm – by now it was dark and raining – a member of staff arriving there with them called together those who were newcomers to the school; you could tell them apart because even those who had spent no more than the previous term at the school had a self-possession lacking in most Jewish children then living in Germany.

You will know him when you see him, Kate told herself, but could not find him.

She was not interested in anyone else. It did not occur to her, as they stood waiting for the local train, that this was the moment for beginning to make friends. Her obsession with finding a boyfriend was something new. She had not had it in Bielefeld, where none of her relationships with boys amounted to more than the slightest of flirtations: not one had kissed her, she had never held hands with one. What prompted her was the need to find an ally, instantly, at the moment when she was being cast into a pit full of strangers. It was a version of finding a substitute Lise, in keeping with puberty.

She had a slight weakness in her ankles, not so much that she needed to wear orthopaedic shoes but enough for her to have had shoes made to measure once when Selma could afford it, because Paul had given her forty marks for her (Selma's) birthday. The tendency of her ankles to give way occasionally made Kate look where she put her feet, which resulted in her not looking at people even when she was standing still, and because of it she was unused to meeting people's eyes casually. Now that she was at the stage of expecting to develop a meaningful relationship with a stranger, she had, as if she were Anne, elevated her habit into a principle: you did not meet anyone's eyes unless you meant something by it. And so, on the short journey from Ulm to the village of Herrlingen, she shook the hands which the other children offered but no more than glanced at their faces, and made no attempt to pair them off in her memory with their names.

A crowd of boys had come down to the station to help with the luggage. All that day, Kate felt, had been leading up to the significant meeting. At first – in her impatience – she had believed that it would happen when she changed trains in Cologne, and then that it would happen as they were travelling beside the Rhine. She had expected to meet him at the station in Ulm; now she felt that time was running out.

And there he was, rather different from the way she had imagined him: he was taller, lanky almost, did not hold himself very well or at least not just then, he was older than she had thought, with dark blond hair falling over eyes so deeply set that she could not make out their colour by the station lights. 'Hi!' he said grinning, when he noticed her watching him. But he also said it to others. She was not certain that he was the one, but no one else there was as nearly right as he.

He pulled the cart on which the suitcases were piled; other boys helped by pushing. She made no attempt to get near him. For the moment, knowing him there was enough. Thinking about him saved her from needing to think, as she climbed among the stragglers, of what was awaiting her at the top of the hill.

There were four buildings set in wooded parkland. They passed the first, which was the Martin Buber House, where Hugo and Judith Rosenthal and other members of staff lived (more rented rooms in the village), and halted in front of the second which was close by. Somebody read Kate's name among others from a list. She was to be in this, the Rambam House. Eighteen boys and girls, no longer juniors but most of them not yet seniors, lived here, in rooms with two or three beds on the first floor. The housemother showed Kate, among others, to her place, a room for three but with only one other occupant, Marianne Holländer, who was one year older than Kate.

'It's the nicest room in the house,' Marianne said. It was, since being at one corner, it had two windows. They had got it by chance but Kate at this stage saw meaning in everything: she was to be privileged because Hugo had once loved her mother. There were a single bed and tiered bunks. As she had had the room to herself, the bed was Marianne's. 'But you can have it if it matters to you,' Marianne said. Being in Herrlingen had that sort of effect on people. Only much later did she tell Kate that she had dreaded the thought of having to share, but from the first had not minded having to share with her. It would have helped Kate to settle down had she known it.

Marianne was a little like Anne; she was as reserved as Anne. It was months before she told Kate that she also had a free place and more than a year before she told her, one day, that she had not always been an only child but had had a younger brother, who had died of meningitis at the age of seven. A painting of him, done posthumously from a photograph, hung in their living-room at home and one day she had come upon her parents standing before it, and overheard her father saying, 'If one of them had to die, I'd rather it had been Marianne.'

She survived the war in England but killed herself soon after it was over.

Kate took the lower bunk. She would have refused to sleep in the upper one, fearing that she would fall out. Later, when it became necessary to adjust to a third girl, it was Marianne who took it. They were consulted about sharing with Leonie, younger than they, whose parents were divorced; it made Kate realize that Marianne must have been consulted. Hugo must have meant her to be a substitute for Kate's sisters and she was; she was the third most important person for Kate in Herrlingen.

The most important, for her as for everyone else, was Hugo: his personality and his convictions made Landschulheim Herrlingen what it was.

Kate had met him, once, when he had in the course of the year come to visit his sisters. Selma had warned her, 'He's extremely ugly.' Judged by conventional standards his face was ugly but that was part of its charm. On that occasion, he had held her hand across the table and told her that she looked just as her mother had done at that age. It baffled Kate that he – her future headmaster! – should have loved Selma, who could not have been very bright: they had met when he had as a student come to supervise her homework. Not until decades later, when they met again in Haifa, did he explain to Kate that this had been her grandfather's way of putting a little money into a poor young man's pocket.

On Kate's first evening in Herrlingen, when she went with the others up to the Bialik House, which was the main building, the people there were already at supper. When they entered the dining-room, Hugo rose to greet the late-comers, but Kate believed that he had risen just to greet her. There were separate tables, each seating ten people including a member of staff or else a senior pupil; the children were divided into social groups, each as mixed as a family, which at mealtimes sat together.

Following the example of the others, Kate went up to Hugo for a handshake. Each meal started (and finished) with the saying of grace – brief except on special occasions – after which there was silence until Hugo announced, 'You may talk.' As the meal was already in progress – and that evening especially people had a lot to tell each other – there was a great deal of noise. It intimidated Kate. She stood there, unsure of herself and bewildered, shadows of tiredness under her big eyes, her heavy brows gathered in a frown: a girl too old for her years who lacked a talent for living, and took herself more seriously than was healthy.

'Where is she going to belong?' Hugo asked someone, meaning to which group. The words touched a raw nerve in Kate and, seeing that she was upset, Hugo got people to make a space for her at his table, opposite him – so that he could look at her, Kate believed, because she looked like her mother. She could barely eat, he was looking at her so constantly, with so much affection.

As an educator, he must have realized, if not at once then soon after, that it was inadvisable to give Kate special attention: it raised her expectations beyond all reason. Her mother used to say of her, 'Offer your little finger and she grabs the whole hand.' During the four terms she spent in his school, he did not concern himself with her further, or so it seemed to Kate, except on two occasions.

When she had been there for about three weeks, he summoned her to the library to remind her that as a lower fourth former she was counted among the seniors, expected to do her homework without supervision in the time between the rest period after lunch and the social hour which began with the late afternoon break. She had been spending that time instead with Kurt Saxl.

Before arriving, even on the train, she had overheard people talking about Gabriel Rosenthal, Hugo's eldest, who had just left Herrlingen for the Land of Israel. Hugo had two other children; other people had left. But it was Gabriel everybody was talking about. He was a brilliant all-rounder altogether beyond control. 'You ought to have known him,' people said, finding words inadequate.

He was Anne's age. He and Kate were never to meet except in the children's pages of the *Jüdische Rundschau*; his drawings of local scenes and his occasional stories appeared side by side with Kate's poems. He trained as a naval officer and was drowned by enemy action off the coast of Sicily, as were all the young Jews on board on their way to fight the Germans.

He had gone to live in Ben Shemen, the children's village about which Kate day-dreamed. When she saw his photograph, she realized that he was the boy whom she had been looking for. From then on she loved him, as she loved Friedemann; what knowledge she had of them supplied her with private legends. He made no difference in her life except in her head.

Being only Kate, she made do in reality with Kurt Saxl.

About ten minutes' walk away, right in the forest, was the Waldheim, housing eight boys and girls from under ten to near adults, who for one reason or another were unable to live at home. Their parents could not afford the Landschulheim fees and they had failed to gain scholarships to it. They attended its lessons – Hugo was not concerned with making money. Kurt Saxl, at almost seventeen, was the eldest. He had already left school and was earning his keep in the Waldheim as its handyman, while arranging his emigration. He was half-Jewish.

Since seeing Kate on her arrival at the station, he had been coming over to the school whenever he could, running all the way when necessary to be there for the long mid-morning break, which she spent at the landing window overlooking the playground, keeping a look-out for him. It was three days before they caught sight of each other. He dashed into the house and up the stairs while she dashed down, until they came face to face. 'I was beginning to think I had only imagined you,' he told her – just what she had been thinking.

After each telling what there was to tell of the search for the other, they could not think of anything else to say. She was relieved when the bell rang. Still grinning, he strode off back to his chores. She returned to her classroom with her face in a fever; people looked at her sideways and showed consideration.

When he had finished his work he came to her house and whistled under her window, that day, the next day, almost every day for the next three weeks or so. On Saturdays they met earlier and for longer. When he was unable to come in the afternoon he sought her out in the mid-morning break, not only to tell her so but because he needed to see her just as she needed to see him. On some days he came then anyway, just to see her. Catching sight of him continued to affect her like an unheralded thunderclap.

On their first walk together, once they had left the grounds and rounded a bend in the road – with none except nature to see them – he placed a hand on her far shoulder. She was wearing an April-thin blouse; there was not much difference to the feel of his palm when he moved it to her bare arm. Then he placed it on her neck, under her hair which at that time she wore shoulder-length and loose; his thumb was over her nape, his fingertips against her ear lobe. Nobody, not her mother, not Lise, had ever touched her like that; no touch had ever before had this effect on her: it passed through her skin into her bloodstream, which spread it through her body down to the backs of her knees. They stopped walking and, without exerting much pressure, he turned her face towards him and brought his mouth down to hers. His head blocked out the sun. They neither of them knew enough to open their lips.

It felt to her as if he were fingering her heart.

Afterwards they walked on with their arms about each other's waist – his felt slender and muscular. They stopped again, and then again, as if obeying the same unheard music while learning each other's signals. They were very solemn about it, and very inhibited.

Kate did not tell him that no boy had ever kissed her; she feared that it would make him doubt her desirability. It did not make her doubt his when he told her that he had never before kissed a girl – an instinct which she had not known she possessed had let her guess it. Her constant, comprehensive ambition to be the first made her rejoice at being his first girlfriend; it allowed her to think a little more of herself.

For a while it seemed to her that he was all she needed, as if she no longer needed her parents and sisters. She saw everyone else in the school as unimportant and by the time she thought of making friends with other people, that year's social life had already cut its grooves.

When it rained, they went to the Waldheim and sat in the outhouse which he had turned into his den, and where, on the walls, there were magazine pictures of Argentina, which was where he was going. They were asking for immigrants willing to become farmers. Kate's father had declared himself willing but had been rejected as too old. She did not mind the thought of Kurt going to Argentina; she was glad that he was getting out of Germany. She was aware that he was right for her only for the time being.

He was not altogether right for her even then. The Waldheim children were seen by the Landschulheim children as inferior. For Kate, the element of slumming was an added attraction; she needed that boost to her ego. The only other friend she managed to make in Herrlingen beside Marianne was Mimi, who was not only also a Waldheimer but a whole two years younger than she. Such a relationship satisfied that part of her conditioned by having Lise. But she was conditioned also by having Anne, which made her aspire to people clearly beyond her reach: Friedemann, Gabriel, and later first one and then another of her teachers. The way she was made, the only relationship which could have satisfied her would have been with someone who would not have wanted it.

Selma, who managed despite the Nazis to make her daughters' childhood such that they were to remember it as having been happy, could not talk to them of sex. She let Kate go off to Herrlingen without explaining it to her. (At the end of the following year she let her leave home for ever without having explained it.) Perhaps Anne could not talk of it either; she did not. And Lise saw it as one of her functions to shield Kate from everything.

Even in Brackwede, Kate had encountered children who 'talked dirty'; her mother's approval then mattering more to her than her own curiosity on the subject, she had walked away from such talk or else closed her ears. By now her mother's approval had ceased to matter to her – or so she believed. But not yet having outgrown her grandfather's influence, she wanted to be approved of by their God. In ancient times, the rabbis, to safeguard the laws of Moses, had put a fence of further laws about them. So now, since Kate was not sure of God's rules, to be on the safe side she ruled all her body below the neck taboo, except for the sort of touching she was used to with Lise.

Thus, the friendship between her and Kurt was unable to develop. They had already on their first walk done everything that was acceptable to her. To her, the spiritual mattered more than the physical. Bodies were circumscribed but there were no limits, she believed, to what one could think and feel. It sufficed for her to walk with Kurt hand in hand or with their arms about each other because to her, their conversations and the forest setting substituted for what else there might have been. When Kurt pressed her to him, front to front, it stopped her from breathing as her nose was squashed against his chest – he was that much taller. It was this her attention focused on, so as to escape all thought of his erect penis against her abdomen. She felt it without knowing what it was.

Subliminally, she knew more than she would admit to herself or could cope with. She had a history of tonsillitis and so, when she got a sore throat, she made so much of it that she was put in quarantine in the infirmary, a purpose-built annex to the Martin Buber House. Here she lay, released from responding to all demands except those she chose to make on herself.

Having learned nothing from her failed friendship with Ingrid – or having forgotten what she had learned or believing that it did not apply – she wrote long, loving letters to Kurt not as he was but as she wished him to be. To give him time to answer before they met again, to sharpen though only his spiritual appetite for her company, she needed to remain in the infirmary, and so she rubbed the thermometer against her palm – totally unaware of the symbolism.

Marianne overheard their housemother talking on the telephone to the matron: Kate's family doctor had not warned them that she was subject to fluctuating high temperatures. She had not always been left alone with the thermometer. Now the matron made a point of not leaving her alone with it.

Kate sought Kurt out in his den and he took her for one more walk. The green of the trees had darkened and all sorts of things were in flower. But he kept his hands in the pockets of his black corduroy shorts which, uniquely, had no swastikas on their fly-buttons (black corduroy shorts were part of the HJ uniform); he had once shown her, much to her embarrassment. He wore his dark blond hair rather long. It was lank and he had a way of tossing it out of his eyes which she no longer thought in keeping with his character. But he was being obstinate now; nothing she could think of saying made any difference. They were not suited to each other, he told her, she was too intense, she had been taking their friendship too seriously: he felt emotionally overwhelmed by her. She ought to find herself somebody of her own age.

She wanted to hear him say that he had ceased to love her, to admit that it was not she but he who had failed. He would not say it. Eventually, he told her that he would be leaving before the end of the month.

In the entrance hall of the Bialik House there was a board on which people exhibited the photographs they had taken, so that others who wished to have copies could order them. Because he was leaving, someone had taken a photograph of Kurt Saxl. Kate did not like to put her name down for it, for all to see. Such a child she was still, feeling so unimportant that she needed to believe herself to be the centre of everybody's attention.

She would have liked to have had his photograph. But she did not need it to remember what he looked like.

Fourteen

When Kate came home for the holidays, she slipped into her place within the family, into her place within the community – but not as if she had never been away. Each three-month absence made her aware, as if she had been absent from herself, that in the meantime she had grown up a little. That was due less to the passage of time than to all the influences of Herrlingen at work on her. When she had made her Hanukkah poem she had certainly been sincere. But she had not known that she felt at all positively about being a Jew, it had surprised her. In a Jewish environment, this feeling rose to the surface. On the one hand, it let her fulfil one of her strongest and most constant ambitions, which was to belong; on the other it supplemented her grandfather's and the Zionist youth movement's teachings.

By the second term, she felt so passionately about the Land of Israel that it won her a long-distance race. Except on the Sabbath and in heavy rain, their day began with the morning run. Kate liked the feel of the early air on her night-warm skin. The children ran from their houses to meet at a fixed point in the forest, and from there they all ran together back to the sports ground in front of the Bialik House for gymnastics, the time for this depending on the length of the route they had come by.

No time for gymnastics was left when they went by the longest route, which therefore they did not take often. One morning, at the meeting place, the teacher announced that they should take it for a race; he had two calendars with pictures of the Land of Israel, which would go to the first boy and the first girl to arrive.

Kate was not good at sport. She had not known how well she could run, nor had anyone else. All that roaming about the fields and forests in Brackwede, all that walking everywhere in Bielefeld to save the tram fare, had strengthened her calf muscles. But what was chiefly responsible for her coming in as the first girl was sheer determination.

It made her a little more popular with the boys; the football captain even tried her out for his team. They never really forgave her for having chosen, as her first boyfriend there, a Waldheimer – and she never had another.

From now on, during the holidays, in Bielefeld, she had a boyfriend, never the same one for long. Not so much because people were constantly emigrating as because she was wilful about it, searching during the first few days for someone on whom to hang her romantic notions, searching urgently because she had only a few weeks.

The most important of them was Hans-Peter Schürmann, the brother of Gisela, whose presence in the bed next to her cot had comforted her in Salzuflen. He was a full nine years older than she and worked at the haberdashery counter in the town's largest department store, which was then still owned by Jews. He was tall and dark and handsome, with an attractively husky voice. After the *Kristallnacht* he escaped to Holland; from there he was taken via the Westerbork camp to Auschwitz, where he died or was killed early in 1944.

He never did more to Kate than stroke her hair and hold her hand; they also kissed. Her feelings for him were strong enough – or she persuaded herself that they were – for her to want to spend more and more time with him. Eventually, she used to wait for him at the end of his working day outside the staff door. They were seen and he was teased by his workmates. Kate looked younger than she was and, next to him, she seemed very small. There was only about a week of her holiday left but he refused to go on seeing her. This was not the only occasion on which her greed for more lost her even what she had.

Lise was also in love with Hans-Peter; that Kate did not know about it until many years later probably means that she was in love with him at the same time. He may even have stopped seeing Kate because he preferred Lise; Kate did not know that boys had begun to find her pleasant to be with. None of what evidence there was of this registered with Kate, so used was she to thinking that she was better than Lise at everything except music.

Usually their taste in boys did not coincide; usually Kate knew with whom she was in love. For a long time, it was with Horst Hauptmann, who was three years older than she and like Hans-Peter escaped to Holland. He was deported to Riga where he did not survive for long. He was the leader of the local Zionists and every girl in the movement was at one time or another in love with him.

Before Kate came home from Herrlingen for the first time, they warned her that, when she did, Anne would not be there. She had found a job in that internationally famous spa Bad Nauheim. It upset Kate, the realization that life had not been standing still for her family while she was away. That Anne had not delayed to await her return. It made her realize that she was right to think herself unimportant. She had not meant to be taken seriously when she thought that.

Anne's employers owned a souvenir shop. She had visualized herself as standing behind the counter, it was at that moment all she asked of life, that chance of contact with the world beyond Germany's borders. She believed she would know how to make use of it.

She was made to do the housework. She did it as if she were Lise. While the days of the season ticked past, she strove to please those strangers more than she had ever bothered to please at home. They had told her, 'If you prove yourself we will let you serve in the shop.' They might have been too commonplace to recognize her worth but they were also Jews, they were also parents with a teenaged son. They ought to have thought about her as well as about themselves. Anne wrote home, complaining.

Paul wrote to her employer and he wrote back that she first needed to learn the business and also, trade was bad. And in any case, he wrote, he could not let Anne serve his customers because of her speech impediment. Had he been told of this he would never have offered her the job.

What speech impediment? Paul, Selma, Lise and Kate asked each other. In all the sixteen years of her life no one had ever before found fault with the way she spoke. She had a slight lisp, a very slight lisp, that was all. Those people! They had been given Anne – not just any girl much too good to serve in their shop but Anne, and evilly they had dared not merely to find fault but to invent one where there was none. It illustrates what the Loewenthals had been reduced to, that they did not write to Anne, did not telephone there and then to tell her that she should come home.

Instead, Selma went to Dr Kronheim – the highest benevolent authority available to her – and got it from him in writing that Anne did not have a speech impediment or that if she had, it was so slight that he, the rabbi, had never noticed it. His letter was, in addition, a character reference.

That was what amounted to a victory among the Jews living in Germany then: that such a girl as Anne was should be allowed to serve behind the counter of a souvenir shop.

At the time when Kate went to Herrlingen, Lise became an apprentice dressmaker with Frau Nathan, who in the days before Hitler had had Selma among her clients. She was still patronized by Aryans and had two Aryan assistants, girls in their early twenties, who talked about their lives and loves in front of Lise as if she had no ears. They treated her kindly.

Frau Nathan treated her kindly, too. But Lise as always invited exploitation. It was she who delivered the finished garments to the customers. 'Be as quick as you can,' Frau Nathan told her, probably from long habit; Lise took the injunction literally and ran all the way there and back. The tips she was given she handed over to be shared out; she thought this only fair and did so even when someone, taking pity on her, told her, 'This is for yourself.'

Her working hours were from eight to six. Selma was always up before her; in the winter she used to light her daughters' stove (the only continuously burning stove was in the kitchen). But Lise did not have the time to wait until the room had warmed up; she used to get dressed under the bedclothes and while doing so fall asleep again and again.

Not even the nicest garments looked nice on Lise, and so it was thought that it did not matter what she wore; it did not matter to her. Combing her silky black hair, she did not even bother to get the parting straight. She did not try, as Anne would have done in her place, to make the best of herself. She had decided early that there was no point because whatever she did she would not look as nice as Anne or Kate.

There was one dress – perhaps that winter it was the only dress Lise had – made of towelling cloth, with narrow horizontal stripes in shades of green and brown, which had press-studs from neck to hem that took Lise's numb fingers so long to fasten that Kate, on holiday from Herrlingen – still able to live as a child – grew impatient watching and called out to her, 'Wake up, Lise!' She herself could feel Lise's sensations, the cold without and the exhaustion within, and willed some of her own energy across to her.

She knew the feel of Lise's bed as well as she did that of her own: from the days when she used to get in with her, to tell stories and to play games. When Lise had been little and suffered from nosebleeds, some doctor had recommended a horsehair pillow; she still used it, it was small and flat and hard. It had not always been Kate who got into Lise's bed because she did not want to have her in her own. There had been a time, before this, when Kate had commanded Lise to come and place her hand against the small of her back, which felt vulnerable – and Lise had lain like that, uncomfortable, motionless, until her little sister had fallen asleep.

According to Selma, she gave up playing the piano because Paul did not care for music, and when their daughters were little they would not sit still to listen but demanded their turn at the keyboard. But there must have been many occasions when, if she had wanted to, she could have played for her own pleasure. Why did she deny it to herself?

She did not encourage even Lise to play. Lise would have preferred to play the violin. When she was still quite little she asked for one and was given a toy. If one is to believe her – and who should know better? – it affected her outlook for the whole of her life. A talent like hers ought to have bulldozed its way out into the open; she lacked the egoism that belonged with it.

Until they entered their teens, anything Lise had Kate had to have too. She also had a mouth-organ and a recorder and, making up in determination for what she lacked in talent, she learned to play them. (She also had ice-skates and roller-skates, but did not feel nearly so strongly about learning to use them.) In the days when they went to the Sarepta school and saved their tram fare, she bought herself not only a wrist-watch but, first, the simplest Hohner accordion. She paid a deposit on it and, denying herself even buttermilk, even liquorice, week after week she paid off the price until it was hers.

She mastered it well enough to have other children dancing the *horrah* (circular dance) to her playing – as long as there was nobody present who really knew how to play. Lise accepted that this was Kate's instrument and never once laid a finger on it even for the purpose of teaching Kate. Kate could not bear to admit in this or any other instance that Lise had anything to teach her.

Lise bought herself a lute. At that year's Hanukkah celebration, she sat by herself, cross-legged on the stage and sang Hebrew songs. The audience loved to hear her and asked for encore after encore. People were still talking about her singing when Kate came home.

So fiercely jealous was Kate that if she could have turned back the clock, she would have chosen to give up Herrlingen for the sake of also having been there that Hanukkah, and also having made an impression on their home community.

As an apprentice dressmaker, Lise was paid no more than pocket-money. Now she could pay for violin lessons – if she had a violin. Friedemann, older and no longer as obtuse about the children, offered to lend her his, and she managed to find a teacher still willing to accept a Jewish pupil and to have her come one evening a week for half an hour – all she could afford. 'It's a shame to neglect such a talent,' he told her.

But before long, the mother of one of his other pupils objected to their having to pass Lise on the stairs. And he had a living to earn. . . .

Kate's first love for making music had been and remained the piano. She could not play it by ear, and so she bought a sheet tutor and taught herself to read music, not giving up until she had mastered the first flats and sharps and had a repertoire of easy pieces. 'You have a hard touch,' her mother said. Even that did not discourage her.

Once Kate had broken the taboo, Lise also started to play, sitting down and improvising so that it sounded as if the wireless were playing. It awed Kate, the music hidden in Lise. But she would not admit it. She would not yield the field to Lise. When their mother ruled that Kate could not play while she was at home to hear her because it gave her a headache, and, to make it fair, that Lise could not play then either, Kate insisted on having her share of the time whenever their mother left the house. That Lise was more in need of making music, that being deprived of it was harder for her, Kate did not understand until years later – and then she blamed Lise for not having explained it to her.

Years later they were to ask each other: why had their mother not said to herself, there is so much which my daughters must go without which I can do nothing about – at least I can teach them to play the piano; or, at least I can teach the gifted Lise; or, at least I can let her or let them play the piano as much as they want – why had their mother not thought that and acted accordingly?

Afterwards, Kate regretted not having chosen for her bat-mitzvah from the 118th Psalm the verse, 'The stone which the builders refused is become the headstone of the corner.' It was how she came to feel about herself, this Jew whom the Germans had rejected would grace her people.

She came to regret having undergone a bat-mitzvah, because to orthodox thinking this was a heathen custom. Dr Kronheim had given each girl a prayer-book inscribed for the occasion. Hers had its own place on the top shelf of the cupboard in the vestibule which housed the prayer-books of the community and, when the synagogue was burned, it pleased her to think that this evidence of past assimilation had been destroyed.

Hugo Rosenthal had his own brand of orthodoxy, resembling that of her grandfather, who could not have settled in Brackwede – twenty minutes by car from the synagogue – if he had not been liberal in his interpretation of the commandments. With her penchant for all or nothing, Kate became more orthodox than that. On Tishah be-Av, commemorating the destruction of the First and Second Temples, she had a row with her housemother because she insisted on sleeping that night on the floor, in mourning.

The only commandment still observed by Selma was the keeping of a set of cooking pots and of tableware for use only on Passover. (As a present for the Jewish New Year in 1937, Lise made her a little box into which she put a morsel of bread, 'so that throughout the coming year we shall always have bread in the house'. Selma pinned it to the side of the kitchen cupboard; they forgot to remove it for the Passover – when Jewish households must be free of leaven – and to the Kate of those days this was a serious transgression.)

The girls had at the time been too small to remember that Selma had ever lit candles on a Friday night. 'I haven't the heart for it,' she said to Kate. 'You do it.' Kate did. She did not always light them herself, she liked Lise to do it; but when she was home from Herrlingen she felt responsible for seeing that they were lit. She asked their father on that night, as a preliminary to their meal, to say the traditional blessing at least over bread – she did not go so far as to insist on wine. 'I don't know the words,' Paul said. She learned them and he said them after her. It was to be many years before it occurred to her that even he must as a boy have learned such prayers; to pretend ignorance would have been his idea of a joke.

By a family tradition dating from the time when all three sisters were still living at home, they always had cake for their Friday evening meal. They could not afford to buy cake as an extra and Selma may have thought that her daughters ought not to be deprived of it altogether; it must have worked out much cheaper than buying meat. Two individual pieces each was the allowance, and the choosing and buying at the confectioner's on the far corner of Theesener Street became part of the ritual.

The bread to supplement the cake was white; the rest of the time they ate rye bread bought day-old, which was cheaper. Selma saved money where she could, thought it worth while to walk all the way into town to buy jam; there was a shop there that sold it loose from a barrel, and you brought your own jar.

There were shops in which she was remembered as having been a good customer in the days before Hitler, where she was still addressed, deferentially, as 'Frau Architekt'. A delicatessen for instance, where an elderly assistant would cut her samples of choice cheeses, conniving in the pretence that she was considering buying.

He once gave Kate a slice of pineapple which was really part of the display, so that she might know how it tasted; she had asked what it was.

But it needed courage to enter such a place: from one day to another you might find yourself no longer welcome. More and more shops were putting up signs saying, 'Jews not wanted'.

Fifteen

Early in 1938 Paul suffered a heart attack.

Kate had been back in Herrlingen for no more than three weeks when she received the letter from her mother which told her of it. He was in hospital and getting better.

Her first reaction was, she is just saying that. If it were true that he was getting better, she reasoned, then why had her mother even mentioned it? They could have told her all about it when next she came home. They must be preparing her . . . and even at this moment, while where she was everything went on as if nothing had happened, he might already be no longer alive.

She had always taken his existence for granted as part of her own, had never given it much thought, had never given him much thought. He had not played much of a part in her life. If she had been asked what her father was like – nobody had ever thought of asking her – she would of course have been able to describe his appearance (clothed) to the minutest particular, but she was not acquainted with the man within, only knew some of his characteristics.

Only a few weeks after this her parents were to register Lise and Kate for Youth Aliyah, which organized the emigration of children to the Land of Israel. It was what Kate wanted, she had clamoured for it, and Kate wanted it enough for it to happen to them both. But all the talking about it that had gone on by now for a full two years had not made her think once that she was thereby orphaning herself. Certainly after his heart attack there was no chance that Paul would ever be able to follow his daughters to where they were going. Yet she thought of it as being no different in kind but only in scale from going to Herrlingen, as if it meant no more than being farther away.

What she thought was that it was her life, not her parents', and that therefore no thought of them need enter into her calculations. She continued to think this even after discovering that even her father – so much less important to her than her mother – was someone without whom she would rather be dead.

That evening, in his flat, Hugo Rosenthal helped her to telephone home. He placed the call, spoke briefly, and then handed the receiver over. At the sound of her mother's voice Kate burst into tears.

She wept so abundantly that she could not speak. It wasn't anything her mother said, the cause wasn't her father. What overwhelmed her was the sound of her mother's voice, or rather its familiarity, reaching her over more than seven hours' distance. What made her reaction so extravagant was that it was unexpected. She had not known that the sound of her mother's voice mattered to her; she had not known that her mother still mattered to her as much as that. The realization of it flooded her with emotion.

Hugo took the receiver from her and spoke on her behalf. He offered it back to her but she ignored it, and he hung up.

'It seems that your father is very much better,' he said.

At that moment, the state of her father's health did not matter to Kate. Had she been told that he was dying, or had she been told that he was already up and about again, it would not have made any difference to her overwhelming need to return home and be held by her mother. Anne was there with her and Lise was there with her; it was as if Kate had not known what she was doing when she exiled herself to Herrlingen, as if she had only just understood that being away from home meant leaving nothing of herself behind, meant the other four still being a family, even without her. She thought of the rest of the family and missed being together with them more than they could be missing her. She missed them so much that it hurt.

Her mother had said, 'Of course Papa would like to see you. But if he saw you standing by his bedside it would make him think that he was dying.'

'She doesn't want me to come home,' Kate said, thinking aloud. It felt like the saddest thing that had ever happened to her. It had been her choice to leave home; it ought to have been up to her when she returned. She had offered to come back and her mother had said, 'No'. Her mother did not want to have her home.

Hugo made her sit down, and after standing over her for a moment, busied himself about the room, giving her time without leaving her alone. After a while she stopped crying and went to her room.

Marianne, like Anne, was quick to understand. She gathered up her books and went out to let her be alone. Kate took those allies of hers, her fountain pen and blank paper, and wrote a follow-up letter to her mother. 'If you really are as I've always believed, you'll understand what I'm feeling,' she wrote, and realized that if her mother did indeed understand her then there was no need for her to explain anything. But she suffered just then from the need to explain herself and so she went on writing, repeating herself, contradicting herself, explaining how she felt, that nobody loved her; she appealed to her mother to love her enough to compensate her for having an unloving mother.

She wrote and wrote and wrote, tears streaming down her cheeks, tears blocking her nose and making it also run. She could not breathe for tears, she could not see for tears, and still she went on writing, not fast enough for the speed at which her thoughts churned out her desperate, childish words.

Just before lights out, Marianne returned; one look at Kate sufficed for her. 'I won't attempt –' she said. 'Just listen to me about one thing. Don't take that letter to the post box until the morning.'

Kate did not post it in the morning either. She tore it up.

Half-terms were marked by lazy days, on which most of the rules were suspended so that people could do as they pleased. You still had to ask permission to leave the grounds – so that the staff would know where to look for you if anything untoward happened; it was always granted to seniors. Kate and Marianne had walked and cycled on borrowed bikes all over the district and as far as Ulm. Kate spent one lazy day by herself in the fields, walking all morning to make a poem, and sitting all afternoon making a pencil drawing of a plough.

On the lazy day of her second summer term – her last in Herrlingen though she did not know this yet – she set out for a walk. Marianne stayed behind to read, but Leonie tagged along. To shake her off, Kate went further than she had intended, through the village and up the opposite hillside. They were hot and tired when they came to a small clearing, and sat down on the heather there.

They had been unaware that they were being followed. When the boys showed themselves, at first they thought nothing of it. The littler once could not have been more than twelve, the bigger one may have been a little older than Kate. He threw himself on her. She did not at once realize what he wanted.

He was stronger than she; she could not get out from under him though she struggled. She called to Leonie for help, but she had sprung up and just stood there, looking on, as did the other boy, who must have understood what was happening though Leonie did not.

'Come on, you,' the boy said to Kate, and started to kiss her, trying to reach her mouth while she was moving her head from side to side. Her attention thus focused, he got his hand under her skirt and pulled her pants. 'Let me do it to you,' he said. 'You, let me in.'

Kate said, 'I am a Jew and we don't do such things.'

The boy raised himself up on his elbows, the better to look at her. 'You're having me on!' But he knew that in that country, in those days, no one who was not a Jew would have claimed to be one. Slowly, reluctantly, he got up; Kate had not realized that his shorts and pants had been round his ankles.

'You would have enjoyed it,' he told her, and spat in her face.

It was all over before she had time to think about it, and knew what it was she had felt against her thigh. To her own surprise, she did not begin to cry; she thought that it would have been fitting but in fact did not feel like it, not having been helpless and not needing comforting but being content, for once, with being the Kate she was. What she objected to most was having been spat at; all the way back to the school she continued to wipe her cheek.

'What did he want?' Leonie kept asking. Kate's response was to walk faster. She felt the need to talk about what had happened, not to explain it but to have it explained to her.

Back in the grounds, she stopped the first woman she encountered, who happened to be a teacher she rather disliked. It was part of Landschulheim practice for relations between staff and pupils to be informal, based on personality and not rank; it made life harder for people like Kate, who believed that striving to be acceptable to others was a kind of dishonesty. The woman may well have resented suddenly being treated by her as a friend just because she needed

156

one. She interrupted Kate to say that she was in a hurry.

'Listen . . .' Kate said, having started to unburden herself and unable to stop.

'But in fact nothing happened.'

That was not how it seemed to Kate. To call the experience nothing made it appear to her even worse than it had seemed at the time, by contrast with nothing. The teacher told Leonie to run along, raising Kate's hopes that now would come something helpful. But all she said was that Kate, by leaving the grounds without permission, had brought the matter on herself.

She said, 'Your housemother is the one for you to talk to about it,' and walked on.

Kate did not tell the housemother, whom she liked but was not close to either. She did not even tell Marianne, fearing that in addition to almost having been raped she would now discover that she was alone in seeing what had happened to her as more than nothing.

Because children came to Herrlingen from so many different schools, they were divided into classes only for the basic subjects. For languages – Hebrew, English, Spanish, French – and for maths, they were grouped according to their knowledge. On her arrival, Kate was a beginner in English; it had been taught in the Luisen school, but she had been excused from the lessons and allowed to continue with French, which she had already done for two years. In Herrlingen, she was encouraged to drop French in favour of English, more useful in what was then the British Mandate of Palestine.

The only language she was interested in mastering was Hebrew, and she would have preferred to study it full time. At least, she argued with Hugo Rosenthal, let me be allowed to drop all other languages including German. Her mother had begun to say to her, 'How can you make poems in the language in which we are being cursed!' She needed the Hebrew to make her poems in. She was not given the choice.

What also made her unwilling to begin to learn English was that there was no one in the school for whom it was the native language. If she could not hope to learn to pronounce it properly, she would never be able to master it, and in that case she would rather not know it at all. She did not like being, at her age, a beginner in a language; nor did she like the teacher who taught the beginners. At the end of her second term, her group was reading about Shirley Temple's life as a film star – her Hebrew group was reading poems by Bialik. She ceased to pay attention and was surprised to discover that even the dunce of the group knew that the plural of child was not childs, as she had thought.

Teachers, as well, were leaving to emigrate. In her last term, her English group was taught by a newcomer: Franz Hammerschlag. Tall and slim, he was not particularly good-looking, but he was newly fledged and unsure of himself and she was in need of someone round whom to spin her romantic thoughts. She sat in her place and spun them while those about her were reading *The Adventures of Tom Sawyer*. When called upon she did not know where they were and when shown did not know how to pronounce the words; she did not know what they meant.

She sat through a term of teaching by this young man and did not learn a thing. At the end of it, at the staff meeting at which her marks were discussed, the others questioned the low grade he meant to give her. They persuaded him to give her another chance.

She expected she knew not what excitement at his summons. Arriving, heart racing, cheeks aflame, she only half heard his explanation. Was it perhaps – let it be! – an excuse to get her alone? But since she did not know what else to do she sat down as told and submitted to being tested again in English.

'How is it,' he asked her at the end of ten minutes or so, 'that I am the only teacher who finds you stupid?'

If her brain had functioned in his presence sufficiently to allow her to answer that, the question would not have arisen; it was not as paralyzed even by Friedemann. Not before, not since, did anybody ever affect her like that. Most likely he was a very ordinary young man. It must have had to do with the stage she had reached in her development.

In her last summer at home, Kate spent much time with Walter, a cousin so distant that later, by themselves, they were not able to work out what the relationship was. But he called her parents uncle and aunt. He also escaped to England, where she married him, chiefly because by then – with Anne interned on the Isle of Man and Lise having gone on to Palestine – he was all the family left within her reach. The marriage did not outlast the war, but it helped her at a time when she was still too young to be altogether alone.

His parents, both actors, were divorced and he was raised by a childless couple who, in the late thirties, became the caretakers of the community rooms – Kate's Onkel Robert and Tante Sophie. Kate's father got him an apprenticeship as a bricklayer. Kate's mother held him up as an example to Anne because he always handed all his wages over to Tante Sophie. But as he was five years older than Kate they hardly knew each other, until after he had lost his job and she had left school. Then they were two who had time on their hands.

He was half-Jewish. He had been baptized and had a certificate to prove it (and was uncircumcised). There were young men in the same position who put on Nazi uniform, and more who denied or at least ignored their Jewishness. Walter chose not to be counted among the Aryans, foreseeing demands being made on him which he would find unacceptable. He was against Zionism, for much the same reasons as Anne had until recently thought valid. He considered all religion absurd. It provided him and Kate with a lot to talk about. He fell in love with her but thought her too young for him to allow it to affect his behaviour towards her.

He was small for a man, lithe and muscular, with dark blond hair and blue eyes. Girls older than Kate considered him attractive. On the Jewish New Year's Eve he caused a stir among them by attending the synagogue; he was there because Kate had challenged him to come. Wearing a hat, he did not look too young to be standing among the men. This was one of the services attended by almost the whole congregation, even in the days before the persecution; the men and boys packed the downstairs and the women and girls packed all three sides of the balcony. The choir of adults was singing and Lise and Kate were sitting with their mother.

'Who is he looking at?' girls whispered, seeing Walter looking up again and again. He even once put his hand to his hat as if to raise it, but then contented himself with a discreet wave. Kate could not help giggling. Lise told her, 'Don't encourage him! Don't you know that he's sweet on you?'

Kate did not believe it: he did not attempt to behave as Kurt had done, or even Hans-Peter, who were the only boys to whose love, such as it was, she had responded. He did not behave like any of the boys who in the course of the years had run after her, and to whom she had remained indifferent. She did not want his love then; but she was not indifferent to him. She saw him as slightly mysterious because of his background, and she admired his courage. He had gone as a scullion on a Swedish vessel to Australia, with the intention of swimming ashore, but they had docked in shark-infested waters. He was planning to return to Hamburg to try again.

For Kate, the Jewish religious rituals stood for that brief best time of her life, her early childhood. The emotions they aroused in her then cut grooves which remained like operation scars, so that she was to continue to respond to them as if she believed in God even when she no longer did.

She would have said that she loved them all equally, but if she had been made to choose just one it would have been a *kiddush* in a *succah*, perhaps because the Feast of Tabernacles was the last communal celebration before she left home.

If there were Jews in Bielefeld who built their own *succah*, Kate did not know them. The one that mattered to her was built jointly by all the youngsters who wished to participate, though the Zionist youth groups were the ones who made themselves responsible for it. It was put up against one wall in the synagogue garden, where not long before Kate and Walter had picked the fruit from the plum trees for their Tante Sophie to make jam for her café. Year after year, it was put up in exactly the same place.

Three sides of it were made of cloth nailed to posts newly driven into the ground for this purpose. It was roofed with branches through which you could see the stars – in accordance with the commandment. It was thickly decorated with all possible fruit and with leaves and flowers, and the direction in which Jerusalem lay was indicated by a poster saying 'east' in Hebrew. In her last three years at home this was designed by Kate.

160

The bread and the wine were set out on a table, to be blessed after the service in the synagogue, when all who wished to be present went round to the *succah*. In the autumn of 1938, Dr Kronheim was in the United States arranging his emigration. There was only Friedemann, though as far as Kate was concerned the 'only' is out of place: there was Friedemann raising his voice in prayer and it was as if that makeshift hut were protection enough against the world beyond the garden, though it was no protection even against the wind and the rain and it was only weeks before the synagogue was destroyed, together with the family life of many, including Kate.

Sixteen

There were now more children registered with Youth Aliyah than the British were willing to admit into Palestine. The Zionist organizations ran farms, where groups of candidates stayed for four weeks, working half the day and spending the other half on learning Hebrew and other cultural activities, under the supervision of youth leaders who, at the end of each course, allocated the available number of immigration certificates to those who in their opinion were most suitable for kibbutz life. The rest were offered places on long-term training farms.

Anne had earlier that year gone to such a farm, because by the time she became a Zionist she was too close to her seventeenth birthday – the upper age-limit – to be considered for Youth Aliyah. She had little chance of getting an adult certificate: they went to the boys and men, partly because only they were believed to be at risk in Germany and partly because they would one day be needed by the Land of Israel as its soldiers.

Even for places in the selection camps there were waiting-lists. It was mid-September before Lise and Kate went to Rüdnitz, which was not far from Berlin.

Not all her homesickness had cured Kate of believing that for her, life would be more enjoyable elsewhere than she found it at home. She often thought of Lise as standing between her and the sun; she did not think much of herself but she thought less of her. Against all the evidence she believed that she but not Lise would be able to take Rüdnitz in her stride.

'I'm much more used to being away from home,' she told Lise on the way. 'I shall look after you.' She was relying on her experience of being in Herrlingen, relying on having learned something from it, relying on that being something which would now stand her in good stead. As if she had not known that Rüdnitz was bound to be an altogether different place, that being there was bound to be an altogether different experience.

As they had so far to travel, they were among the last to arrive. Those coming from Berlin – about half of the almost forty youngsters – were already known to each other; the rest had already had time to become acquainted. Kate instantly felt that she was an outsider, had made a mistake in coming, regretted being there.

A small, fat ebullient girl – who turned out to be no one special – took charge of them and, showing them to where they could leave their suitcases, on the way explained the layout of the farm, their timetable there and, in passing, introduced them to people. It would have taken Kate days to know as much, and to behave like that was totally beyond her.

'We must put our best foot forward,' the girl said, 'to be among the ones who make it.' Until that moment, that she might not manage to be among those had not occurred to Kate, and she rejected the possibility. With an arrogance that she did not know was part of her character she thought, as good as *that* girl I most certainly am.

The dormitories, two for the boys and two for the girls, had bunk-beds, and sacks stuffed with straw for mattresses; all the lower bunks were already taken. 'As sisters you aren't allowed to sleep in the same room,' somebody said as Lise and Kate looked round and then looked at each other. Rescue me, Kate's look said.

If it occurred to Lise that it mattered what impression they made, that here and now it mattered more than elsewhere at other times, it did not make her give up her habit of shielding Kate. There was no lower bunk left in the other dormitory either. 'She suffers from dizziness,' Lise lied (it was a sense of insecurity Kate suffered from), 'will one of you please, please, give up your place to her.' It did not even surprise Kate that someone did. She was grateful to Lise but also cross with her: Kate expected to have allowances made for her while refusing to admit even to herself that this was so.

Perhaps some of the other girls were more like her than she knew; they wanted Lise to be a big sister to them, too. '*Och*, we want you to stay in here with us,' they told her, instant affection for Lise making them cock a snook at the course leaders, whose opinion of them would determine their futures. Whoever had the bunk above Kate's moved out of it without even being asked.

There were two permanent members of staff: Bernhard, the farm manager, and Liesl, the housekeeper. They belonged to the Zionist centre party and therefore had next to nothing to do with this course run by a party a little to the left (the only party available in Bielefeld to those wishing to join the Zionists); it supplied its own two youth leaders.

Hans, ranking senior, was in his late twenties but looked older; he was still recovering from an operation for stomach ulcers. He was small and slightly built, with a thin, pointed face, a sweet smile, and eyes that matched Lise's. He seemed quiet and unassuming – perhaps more so than he was by contrast with Heinz, who was younger, stocky, and handsome with spectacular auburn hair and eyes of the same rare colour. Kate thought him a smasher.

The farm was licenced by the Nazis – who had not yet thought of getting rid of the Jews by killing them and were encouraging their emigration. Those attending the course were not allowed out of bounds; they were not allowed to discuss German politics or to listen to the wireless – though Bernhard owned one to which the youth leaders listened. On the other hand, their nearest neighbours were beyond shouting distance and the youngsters could sing their Hebrew Zionist songs as much and as loudly as they pleased.

For work they were divided into groups, the composition of which was constantly changed so that all of them would get to know each other. Those who passed the course were to emigrate together, with Heinz as their leader, and after spending two years on a kibbutz would leave it to establish their own. All were expected to work at one time or another at every job. But jobs such as tending the boiler and driving the tractor were as a matter of course left to the boys; it was always a girl who – under Liesl's supervision until she fell ill – was in charge of the kitchen. For Hebrew and Jewish history they were divided into classes according to their attainments.

On their first evening, after the meal, the tables were pushed aside and the chairs placed in a circle, and there was singing until those

164

detailed to do the washing-up had finished and could join in. Then the youngsters, one after the other, introduced themselves. Most likely Kate was not the only one unable to listen for wondering what to say when her turn came. She wanted to make herself known, but even more she wanted people to accept her. She believed – experience had taught her – that the one excluded the other. Because she had all her life been given reason to think well of her looks, her brains, she was unaware of seeing herself as a lesser child. She would have disputed that she was unsure of herself; what she knew herself to be unsure of was knowing how to behave.

Over-estimating the importance of the occasion, she was unable to make use of it, said almost nothing, while looking round the circle of faces with her large, solemn eyes, giving the impression that she was unwilling to cast her pearls before swine, and this without knowing it.

Thanks to Herrlingen, she was in the top Hebrew group, which was taught by the flashy Heinz. One morning, after they had already been there for several days, he mentioned some song and asked, 'Do any of you know it?' – 'I do,' Trude, from Schweinfurt, began to sing it in a contralto voice so beautiful that the rest of them held their breath. What impressed Kate most was that she had not vaunted her gift, as Kate if she had had a voice like that would have done. Kate resolved there and then never again to advertise the talent she had for making poems but to wait, like Trude, until the opportunity arose for others to find out about it.

Quite possibly even before being able to put names to faces, the two youth leaders had shared out the youngsters between them, and it so happened that Kate had fallen to Heinz. When he asked her to come for a walk with him, she forgot his real importance in her life – her future depended on what he thought of her – and promised herself that this was an opportunity she was not going to waste.

They walked through the fields on a warm, still, late September evening, at first in silence. There were some poplars ahead and Kate thought, when we reach them I'll say . . . But before then, Heinz asked her to tell him how she saw herself.

165

She could not do it; it was something she did not know or rather, her opinion of herself differed, depending on who she was with and on her frame of mind – and this depended on when she had last made a poem and whether or not she had been satisfied with it. So as not to remain silent and seem stupid – oh yes, she saw herself as intelligent, but she wanted to demonstrate this, not merely to say it – she began, 'I'm very interested in books, I read a lot.'

There were several shelves of books in the common room. 'Name some of them you know,' Heinz said. 'I haven't seen you reading.'

She had not even looked at them; one of her reasons for loving to read was that it could make her forget the world and she had been doing her best to be sociable. She might have scored points with that answer but did not make it for thinking, he's been observing me! Of course he had; but she mistook his motive.

'Have you read . . .?' he mentioned a title.

She had heard of it; it was a very well-known book for adolescents. But instead of saying, truthfully, I prefer what's written for adults, she came out with, 'That's one of the few books which I haven't read.' Before she had finished speaking, she realized that this was a preposterous statement, but she believed that it would make a worse impression if she were to retract it. Not to give him time to think about it, she quickly began to talk of poetry, and instantly felt better about herself.

'Have you read Rilke's *Cornet*?' she asked him, and he answered her promptly, with a tight-lipped smile, 'That is one of the few books which I *have* read.' What she hated most of all was people making fun of her.

For a moment longer, they looked at each other. The setting sun was behind them, putting orange lights into his stunning hair. She laid claim to being the opposite of superficial, but she judged people by their appearances. It was because of his colouring, she was to realize later, that she had loved Heinz.

He asked her, 'Do you have a boyfriend, Kate?' and when she did not answer at once – her heart frisking – rephrased the question. 'Have you already had boyfriends?'

Now she hated herself for having known no better than not to save herself for someone like him – for him. His like, she believed, did not exist anywhere. But with her history, she needed further encouragement before she could put her feelings for him into words.

He prompted her with, 'Tell me more about yourself.'

Did he mean, on that subject? she wondered. At the time, she did not understand how the process worked, and found fault with herself for being fickle, because no sooner did she cease to be in love with a boy, or was separated from him (which amounted to the same thing), than she found another with whom to fall in love; she needed always to be in love with someone. And the feeling was cumulative: with every next boy she felt all she had felt before plus that little bit extra which made her believe that this time it was the real thing, that here was the one whom she had been loving her way towards all her life. What she was really doing was rehearsing, developing her capacity to love. Which made it no less hurtful to her self-esteem when she was rejected.

She did not feel lovable. She accepted that with her looks – for which she could take no credit – some boys found her physically attractive; for this she despised them as superficial although she, too, could find herself physically attracted. As if the body housing her were extraneous, like a book-cover, and not an organic expression of what was within, she did not value the love it aroused; the self for which she wanted to be loved was represented for her solely by abstractions. These, as she saw it, manifested themselves in the fruits of her mind. What she really wanted to be loved for was her writing, even then.

She did not mention it because of her resolve to learn from Trude. In time this was to result in an inhibition, almost as if she believed that mentioning her poems would take her gift for making them away from her.

She, who believed herself to be so different from everyone else, yet drew conclusions from herself about others. Because she could not see Lise as sexually attractive, it did not even occur to her that she might be to someone else. She believed that Lise still told her everything – it may never have been true – and, conversely, she believed that anything she did not know about Lise could not be. She knew that Lise had fallen in love with Hans, but had no idea that those two had developed a relationship which broke every youth leader's cardinal rule: not to become emotionally involved with one of his charges. Moreover, Hans was married and a father.

When the housekeeper Liesl fell ill, Lise was the only one capable of replacing her in the kitchen, and she did. It meant that Kate, whose turn had come to work there, had to go back to helping with the potato crop. It also meant that Lise came to be regarded by the youth leaders as one of themselves, and kept their hours. When it was lights out in the dormitories, she was still downstairs, drinking a last cup of cocoa in the office, on many nights alone with Hans. They shared among other things a love of music; there was a gramophone there on which Hans played Wagner, Lise agreeing with him that what mattered was the man's music and not his opinions concerning the Jews.

Experience had taught the youth leaders to celebrate the end of the course in advance of letting the youngsters know their assessment. At the beginning of the last week, Heinz asked all who wished to contribute to the entertainment – he hoped that all would – to let him know what they wanted to do so that he could draw up a programme. Kate would have liked to recite one of her poems. It had become known that she wrote them; someone had seen one in the *Jüdische Rundschau*, but it had not made the difference she had expected it to make in people's attitude towards her.

'You suggest it,' she told Lise.

The least she had expected was that Heinz would speak to her about it; since their one walk together he had avoided having anything to do with her – or so it seemed to Kate. But Lise came back with merely the message that he needed to see her poem before he could decide whether or not she should recite it. She chose one from the collection in her head and wrote it out. Taking it into the office, she found Trude there; she had been recruited by Heinz as his secretary, and was typing.

And how had he discovered that Trude could type without at the same time discovering that Kate could also do so? As so often before, she had been unaware of things going on around her.

She watched Heinz for a sign that he had read her poem and that it had made him recognize her worth. When the programme was put up on the notice board, almost everybody's name was on it except her own. He could not have read her poem, it must have got lost among other papers, perhaps by Trude and perhaps on purpose. She rushed to find him.

Surrounded by people, he was perched on a wall in the sunshine and as always, the sight of him caught her by the throat. She sounded as if she had been running when she asked her question, breaking into the conversation which was going on not because she thought herself more important – that was the impression she must have given – but because her feelings just then were too powerful for her self-control.

He told her, 'Your poem is too serious, it doesn't fit in.'

Trude's singing was also too serious. But she took part, her performance was the high-spot of the programme. She told jokes and clowned until everybody except Kate was convulsed with laughter.

She was jealous of Trude also because she would rather have had Trude's talent than her own, not only because singing was more universally appreciated but also because Kate thought less of what she could do and more of what she couldn't.

The group of almost forty youngsters had been allocated twenty immigration certificates.

'So you see,' Hans told them as they sat in a circle in the common room on the final evening, 'we were forced to be very selective, we had to exclude some to whom this is hardly fair; who, if there had been more certificates, would certainly have been passed.' He went on to say that nobody had failed. Those unable to leave Germany more or less at once would be allocated places on training-farms.

Kate had stopped listening before he had finished speaking, when she realized – as she had not done before – that there was a real possibility that she would be failed. She looked round the circle to count the certainties; she did it heart thudding and fingertips freezing, as frantically as if she were practicing magic. The names were read out alphabetically. At each pass she flinched at this diminishing of her chances, wishing now that she had not been so rash as to submit herself to this ordeal. She thought it unfair that throughout the four weeks they had been left to behave as they pleased without guidance. Now, only now did she realize that the fact that not Heinz, not Hans, had ever criticized her did not mean that they had found no fault. Through her mind flashed a hundred and one occasions when she could, when she now knew she ought to have behaved differently.

She thought that probably they would not grant two certificates within one family. Her assumption that she stood a greater chance than Lise was based on the fact that not Lise but she had been given a place in Herrlingen, and also on wishful thinking. Lise, she believed, would be better able to cope with being rejected. Lise – that one had always encouraged her to believe – was able to accommodate herself to anything.

K coming before L, she heard that she had been passed, and instead of relief then experienced a moment of utter panic. Her luck could not hold – and what was the good of anything if it deprived her of Lise?

Hans had asked Lise's opinion of the girls about whom he had been undecided. Late one evening in the office, with the feeling that they were the only ones left awake, he had told her, 'I have my doubts about Kate.'

The love she felt for him had been foremost in her mind. It ceased to matter the moment she was needed by her little sister. 'What doubts?' she asked, no longer his friend.

'She's a good and willing worker. But she doesn't know how to relate to people, she's a born outsider, it would make problems to have her on a kibbutz.'

Lise pretended not to take his words seriously. She did not want to be separated from Kate but that was not what motivated her: she knew that to be rejected by Youth Aliyah would be so damaging to Kate that it would scar her for life. Hesitating only to find the right words, she lied – she would not have lied to him on her own behalf – 'I don't know what's been the matter with her, she isn't usually like this, she hasn't been doing herself justice.'

And so on, until Hans said, 'You know her better than we do, if you think . . .'

Decades were to pass before she judged Kate mature enough to be told the truth.

Before returning to Bielefeld they spent three days in Berlin with Paul's sister and her family. The time was too brief to become acquainted; they had another reason for wanting to stay. Those of their Rüdnitz group who lived there were going to meet at somebody's house towards the end of the week and Kate especially could not bear the thought of them doing this without her, who also belonged.

There was something else she wanted to do, even more important to her. Before going to Rüdnitz, that summer with so much time on her hands – Anne away from home and Lise working – she had written a novel. She did it sitting in Anne's part of their room, on Anne's chair and at Anne's table, writing every day for three hours first thing in the morning for five weeks, and spending much of the rest of the time thinking about it.

It was the title of a book she had not read, *The Little Prophet*, which had captured her imagination. Her little prophet was a peasant boy in biblical Jerusalem, whose pet bull-calf had been taken to be sacrificed in the Temple; he recruited a gang of children who set about rescuing him. If the story was a parable she was not aware of it.

The rejected manuscript was waiting for her at home. Selma had not mentioned it in her letters so as not to upset her while she was away. Under the impression that the publishers had not yet reached a decision about it, Kate's hopes grew like Jack's beanstalk.

She needed her Berlin relations' help to find the address. She must telephone first, they told her, and make an appointment. She did not want to do that, did not want to establish this most important contact in the whole of her life so far by such impersonal means. Besides, she did not know whom to ask for or what to say. They might have told her not to come, and she wanted the experience of visiting a publisher. It was Schocken, as far as she knew the only Jewish publishing house left in Germany.

The entrance was shabby, the inside dark, or perhaps so only by contrast with her bright expectations. At reception, she gave her name across the counter and said, 'As I happen to be passing through

Berlin . . .', a grand phrase rehearsed in thought all that morning. She was told to sit down while waiting, but preferred to remain standing, poised.

The stairs were narrow and winding. Perhaps they only seemed like that to her because to her the place was an enchanted castle. Books everywhere. Paper for books in the making. People whose purpose in life was the making of books as it was her life to write them.

A young woman had come down to take her up. Kate, belonging to a generation which still took for granted that all the important positions were filled by men, mistook her for a secretary; she was one of the firm's readers.

She was concerned to be faced with an enquiry about a manuscript which had already been returned. Kate interpreted her concern more personally, believed that it was for her because of what she had written, believed that it was for her book because of what it was. The woman told her that because it had been a handwritten manuscript, they had feared that it might be the only copy, and returned it by registered post.

This evidence that it had been treated as something of value softened the effect on Kate of the rejection; instantly she felt that she had known all along that the book would not be published, was in fact not publishable, felt that she had never expected to achieve with it more than to be standing in this office with this woman in friendly conversation as between equals. She abandoned her creation, sought refuge with strangers, joined the rejectors to escape feeling that it was herself who had been rejected. Needing to explain how it came about that she did not know that the manuscript had been returned helped her to cope with the moment. What also helped was the conditioning she had been receiving since Hitler had come to power that all she most wanted was beyond her reach.

She had achieved more than seemed to her then. The registered parcel awaiting her at home included a letter from Dr Georg Gross, then one of the directors of Schocken. What plans did she have for her future? he asked. If she needed help, she should let him know; he might be able to arrange her emigration.

It was the sort of letter for which her father had been waiting for years. 'What has he ever done to make anybody want to help him?' her mother asked whenever one of his emigration schemes came to naught. Well, she had done something to make somebody want to help her. It so happened that her emigration was already arranged. But for the rest of her life, the memory of that letter helped her, a little, to cope with the guilt she felt over having survived.

Seventeen

They were in Rüdnitz when Chamberlain met with Hitler; they were there when the Germans annexed the Sudetenland. On that morning, early, they walked on grassland in a long line of girls which had formed on either side of Lise, arms linked, faces towards the rising sun, towards the rosy and orange horizon. It was very peaceful – the chill air on their warm skins – and all they could hear was birdsong. They were waiting for it to be time for them to return to the house and be told the news, just this once though it was forbidden. To them, young as they were, politics was the most burning topic of all.

Selma had been saying for some time that only war could put an end to Hitler. Now Lise said, 'If there were going to be fighting it would already have started and it hasn't, I can feel it.' Lise's mystic side was an embarrassment to Kate. It baffled her that people, always so ready to make fun of her, did not also make fun over this in Lise.

They were back in Bielefeld when, at the end of October, the Germans rounded up and expelled all the Jews who at one time or another had come from Poland and for various reasons failed to change their nationality. They were taken east in a rehearsal of the later mass deportations, but the Poles did not want them either and so they were left, under appalling conditions, abandoned in no man's land.

Kate, who had been writing to Heinz, restricting herself to one letter a week or so and to expressing her ideas and not her feelings, received a rare postcard from him which said among other things that Jo was in Poland. If she had been able to heed her natural inclinations and not felt constrained to love beyond her reach in order to shore up her self-esteem, she would have loved Jo, who had made eyes at her until discouraged by her lack of response. Or perhaps what prevented her from loving within her means, so to speak, was fear of failure. That Heinz would not find her adequate, would not love her as she loved him, was only to be expected. But supposing Jo had loved her less than she him, had found her inadequate – then what would she have had to think of herself?

He was physically not unlike Gabriel Rosenthal, or rather he was like her imagined Gabriel, with curly dark hair and phenomenally nice eyes and a sense of humour to make up for her seriousness, one who could make others laugh without being laughed at. Or perhaps her lack of response had been due simply to her fear of her own sexuality. Jo, unlike Heinz, would have cuddled and kissed her; he was not one who could have been stopped, she would not have wanted to stop him.

And now he was in Zbonszyn. Now the constellation of circumstances was such that she loved him so much that it hurt.

Theesener Street was long and straight – you could see the postman coming. Lise had, after Rüdnitz, resumed her dressmaking, while Kate was once more on holiday, but she got up as early for the sake of receiving the post. She would go out to meet the postman. When he did not object to being stopped by her and asked to look if there was anything for the Loewenthals, she went a little further each morning, until she was meeting him at the corner of the main road where the trams ran, and where there was a *Stürmer* display case, inciting every German against every Jew.

On most mornings there was nothing for her, and only bills for her father. 'What important letter can a little girl like you be waiting for?' the postman eventually asked her.

'Permission from the British to enter Palestine,' she answered.

On the morning of the Tenth of November, a Thursday, Kate and her mother went up the three flights of stairs to the attic, where there was a large open space with clothes-lines to dry the washing in bad weather, and every family had a lock-up lumber-room. Earlier that year, householders had been commanded to clear these out, because in the event of the rest of the world once more making war on Germany – it was predicted – the lumber represented a fire hazard. Under the circumstances, the rag-and-bone men were in the position to charge Jewish householders in particular for carting it away. Selma nevertheless managed to find an old man with a donkey willing to oblige her for nothing. Another turned up, claimed to be a partner, and made off with the spoils. When the first old man turned up, Selma felt so badly about having allowed herself to be tricked into breaking their agreement that she found some things which were not rubbish at all to give to him – though she was as poor or more likely poorer than he.

Among the things which remained was a trunk full of clothing, mainly Selma's from the days before Hitler: fine silk dresses, evening gowns, furs – too elegant for her present existence – things which, like her piano, she held on to, to help her pretend that she had faith in the future. There were also some of Anne's old clothes which Lise was not thought to need and Kate had not yet grown into, and clothes which had been given to them in charity waiting to be made over.

Lise had by then served a year and a half of her apprenticeship and was expected to make most of her own clothes. She was able to do so, but as she was unwilling to spend what little spare time she had on sewing, she made do with the minimum, convinced as she was that it did not matter what she wore. Yet she was better off than Kate, who believed that only while she looked nice would people like her, and that looking nice would be the only thing they would like her for. Kate had far more clothes because she had needed them in Herrlingen, and also because Selma liked making things for her. It was to find things which could be made over for her that they went up to the attic.

Kate liked to be given things, no matter what, even a piece of liquorice or a cigarette card; her pleasure was in the getting. Of greatest value to her was what was given by Anne – obviously, it was emotional satisfaction rather than possessions she was after. Something inherited from Anne – including toys and books – was always preferable to something new. She was delighted with her haul that morning, an armful of clothing almost too heavy to carry down the stairs.

She was behind her mother, who stopped when the last turn brought their front door in sight: an elderly woman, a stranger to Kate, was standing there. She was dressed all in black and weeping.

Selma's first thought was that something had happened to Paul and she almost fainted.

'No, no,' the woman said, 'he is all right, he sent me.' He wanted them to come into town, to Tante Hete's house; he thought that they might not be safe where they were, the only Jews in the neighbourhood. That night the synagogue had been set on fire.

She had said all this before they had reached the kitchen, which they did slowly, moving awkwardly down the narrow corridor, with Selma supported between the stranger and Kate. Kate's support was only half-hearted: she was still too young to adjust quickly to this reversal of roles. They sat Selma down and the stranger, as if the place were her own, brought her a glass of water. 'That I should live to see this day!' Selma exclaimed. These words when said in Hebrew conclude the prayer used to thank God when encountering a blessing.

Both mother and daughter were dressed too shabbily to go visiting as they were. To change, Kate felt, detracted from the drama of their situation, but she did as she was told. The flat was not ready to be left, they had not yet done all the morning chores. It felt like flight to Kate to leave it thus and at a moment's notice.

The stranger waited for them although Selma tried to send her ahead, delayed on purpose because she wanted to be rid of her, was as ashamed to be seen walking with her as Kate was ashamed on that day to walk with her mother. Both women were identifiable as Jews, even though their features were not explicitly Jewish. They looked not merely like mourners but like victims. Paul's advice had been not to take the tram; in fact, the new laws issued on that day forbade Jews to use public transport and also ordered them to give way to Aryans on the pavements by stepping into the gutter. Before they had gone the length of Kügler Street – not a long nor a busy street – they were obliged to step aside for a man. They did not yet know of the new law, but acted accordingly when he spat at Selma, his spittle landing on the hem of her coat.

At the far end of the street in which Tante Hete lived was the Kesselbrink, an open tree-lined square from which the buses ran. (Including those which took the Jews from a hall there, which served as their assembly place, to the railway station. Those buses ran from

December 1941 onwards, until there were no Jews left in Bielefeld except some young slave labourers in a small camp.) On the far side of the Kesselbrink was the fire station, at the corner of Turner Street. A short distance down Turner Street was the synagogue, on the left; on the right were an old cemetery and a police station.

But from outside Tante Hete's house, by the time they got to it there was no sign of the fire.

The front door remained unanswered, remained closed. The woman who had brought them went round to the servants' entrance at the side, and came back to fetch them. Saying, 'Quick, quick', she dragged Kate by the hand. The people within – twenty or more – groused at Selma and Kate though all they had done was to linger by the front door. Kate felt that for some reason they were not welcome; the Jews were not welcome to one another on that day and yet they congregated. There was danger in numbers, they infected each other with fear, and rumours bred rumours. While remaining just as defenceless, they felt as if they were strengthened by community.

There was already standing room only, except in the kitchen where Selma was taken by some other women because she was feeling faint from lack of air, or from the noise of conversation held in whispers, but seeming loud because there was so much of it, with such urgency in the tone. Or perhaps she felt faint with disappointment because Paul was not there. And perhaps his absence was the reason why they were not welcomed. On that day, no Jew wanted to be with another on whose behalf he needed to fear or to grieve more than he did on his own.

The centres of attention – or it may just have seemed so to Kate – were her Tante Sophie, and Walter's sister Ruth. They had been rescued from their flat above the community rooms when these were already on fire. It seems unlikely that the local Nazis had not known they were there; the fact that they were not warned to get out perhaps confirms what Paul was to be told: that the men who set fire to the synagogue were brought by lorry from outside Bielefeld, because even the Nazis there refused to do such a thing.

They had had to jump to safety and Ruth had broken her arm. Onkel Robert had been arrested. Walter was in Hamburg and the two women kept saying how lucky this was for him – no one in the room yet knew that throughout Germany and Austria the synagogues were burning and men were being arrested. (Walter came back that night to see if there was anything he could do for his family. Tante Sophie insisted on his returning at once to Hamburg, where he could pass as an Aryan because nobody knew him.)

There had been other arrests in Bielefeld, and Kate's reaction to the talk of Walter was to think, what does he matter? As if he were not her cousin, as if he were unknown to her, as if he were not a human being. Suddenly she was seeing the Jews as the Nazis saw them; the years of indoctrination had finally taken effect. Her indifference – beginning on that day – was confined to the men, and it included her father. The only thing about him which still mattered was that he was a Jew and Jewish men did not matter.

Just then she would not have cared about it had she known that Friedemann had also been arrested. He had run into the burning synagogue with the thought of saving the scrolls, and fought the Nazis who had run after him to prevent this. He was one against several who had weapons and he had none. With no chance of success, he fought on without fear until they had beaten him unconscious.

The people in Tante Hete's house left, each for his own reason; others came, there continued to be as many. That Selma and Kate were relations made a difference – or it may just have seemed so to Kate. She was called into the kitchen, given a plate with bread and butter and a piece of cake, and urged to get her mother also to eat something, before they left, 'or she'll faint in the street'. And Kate, who had so often wished Lise out of the way so that she could have their mother to herself now wished either that Lise were there or that she were not there. Tante Hete had phoned Frau Nathan to tell Lise to stay where she was.

Someone who had just come had brought a message from their father: they were to meet him at the flat of Hugo Rosenthal's sisters, which was beyond the synagogue on the way to the castle. 'Don't go through Turner Street,' the women told Kate, as if she and not her mother were to be responsible for them both. They gave her conflicting advice about what route to take, recognizing that she was still too young for the task. She did not listen to them, convinced that she knew and loved Bielefeld better than they or anyone else did, including all Aryans. She had no intention of agreeing to a detour even should her mother wish to make one: there was nothing which mattered to her so much at that moment – not even finding her father – as seeing what had happened to the synagogue. She was a glutton for dramatic events.

The day had turned colder and greyer – or it may just have seemed so to Kate. She linked arms with her mother; they were now the same height and Kate was to grow no taller. They crossed the Kesselbrink. Selma and Paul were to be among the first eighty-eight Jews from the town deported eastwards; they were not among the six survivors from that transport.

They walked at a pace natural to those who know where they are going but are not in a hurry; they did not want to attract attention and did not expect to meet Paul for almost another hour. Anxiety about him had made Selma set out much too early and now made her choose to go by the shortest route. They passed the synagogue at the same pace. There were no spectators, only here and there people who looked as if they, too, happened to have a destination which led them through that street.

The large central dome had gone, as had the smaller domes on the four corner towers, but the blackened stone walls remained up to about two-thirds of their height. Shards from the stained glass windows had been blown on to the pavement. There were no longer any flames, but smoke was rising in billows as if the ruins were breathing. In passing, Kate picked up a small piece of sea-green glass and, putting it in her coat pocket, wondered which of the traditional short blessings, each beginning by praising God, she ought to be saying.

Hugo Rosenthal had three sisters, Rosalie, Grete, and Alma. Alma had once been one of Selma's closest friends. In the spring of 1939 the sisters emigrated to Holland; Alma died in Sobibor and only Grete, living in hiding, survived the war.

Grete was not then living in Bielefeld. Kate had been to the flat where Alma and Rosalie lived – Selma had taken her to it to meet Hugo, coming with her no further than the courtyard. Selma explained, when they got there (and Kate, still not understanding the situation, needed the explanation), that Paul had chosen this meeting place because the Gestapo were less likely to come to an address known to house only women.

They climbed the three flights of dingy stairs – shared lavatories on the half-landings – and found the front door already ajar for them. On her previous visit, Kate had been full of herself and the occasion – a scholarship girl meeting her future headmaster. She had paid no attention to her surroundings which anyway were not Hugo's but his sisters'. Forgetting that she was more than a year and a half older, she believed that it was the effect of the day which now made her take notice of the good furniture crammed into too little space, the genteel destitution. It did not smell of poverty like this in Kügler Street. She had been into as poor or poorer homes, but never on errands connected with her father. It was waiting for him in the Rosenthal's flat that made her think of him objectively for the first time.

They waited and they went on waiting, in vain. The three women sat together, facing each other; Kate felt excluded as much by their silences as by their conversations, and also by their shared memories. They had placed her at a small round table by the window, so that she would have light by which to read, and given her a leather-bound volume of the collected works of Goethe. At any other time, this tacit recognition of her status would have pleased her but she did not want it then because she did not want to have to live up to the responsibility; it made her feel as if she were the only one who was visiting there, made her feel alienated from her mother.

Drinking tea – served in bone china cups – did not help to pass the time but, done repeatedly, made it seem longer. Selma ought to have been used to Paul not coming when he said he would. He was by nature unpunctual, always preferring other men's (and other women's?) company to going home. On many occasions when he was expected back for lunch and was late, Selma said, 'He has no consideration.' Kate used to believe that she was referring to the food spoiling, and Selma let her believe it; she did not want to burden Kate with knowing that she constantly feared for him. Since their courting days, he had been in the habit of announcing himself by whistling the opening bars of the folk song, 'Comes a little bird flying'. At this signal, Selma would turn to the cooker and begin to serve up, not letting Kate see her tears of relief, and Kate would think that she cared too much about her cooking, which had not been special even in the days when she had been able to afford the choicest ingredients.

Two o'clock, he had said. Alma almost succeeded in persuading Selma that he had said not two but three (the numbers sounding very similar in German). When that time had passed she called Kate into the kitchen. 'There must have been a misunderstanding,' she told her. 'Go back to your Tante Hete.' She should slip out quickly, without telling her mother, who would only try to stop her. And Kate, who had reached the stage of believing that she had outgrown her mother, instead of feeling more adult, was made aware of still needing her mother's approval before she did anything.

Alma had got out her purse. Perhaps her fingers were made clumsy by the responsibility she was taking upon herself; the trouble she had finding the right coins made her appear unwilling to part with the money. 'Take the tram,' she said, 'only be quick or your mother's heart won't stand it.' Kate thought that she meant it literally, and believed her.

There was no convenient tramline from the one place to the other; Kate thought her feet would be quicker. Back she ran to Turner Street and along it. Just before she reached the synagogue she crossed a side street down which, at a distance, she saw an open lorry, with some men on it and others climbing up, and uniformed Nazis standing by. She stopped for a longer look, but did not dare to approach, not out of fear for her own safety – the killing of Jewish children (and women) had not yet started – but because she feared finding her father there and being confronted with his helplessness and with her own.

Sure only of being uncertain, she ran on.

Never had she run so fast for so long, not even in Herrlingen on the morning run that had won her the picture calendar. Perhaps this running was made an ordeal by fear: that she would not be able to find her father, that she would not find him before her mother's heart could no longer stand the waiting. Fear that she would come upon something even worse than the burned synagogue, the lorry with the men. Her throat ached, her lungs ached, she had a stitch in her side. And still she ran on just as fast; that she could do it was some consolation.

182

Why had Alma not told her to find the nearest public telephone? Kate would not have been convinced that it was her father she was speaking to, even hearing his voice, and her having heard his voice would not have convinced her mother. And if he was not at Tante Hete's, she could not have found out over the telephone where else he might be. Using the telephone would not have saved time, but wasted it.

At Tante Hete's side door, she forced herself to knock gently so as not to cause alarm. 'Who is it?' someone called out, and it was a moment before she had gathered breath enough to speak her name. The door was opened by a woman she did not know but who knew her. With an intonation as if she believed that Kate had come merely by accident, she told her, 'Your father is here.'

She could already see him, because among Jews he stood – like King Saul – head and shoulders above other men. It was as if she had not seen him for a very long time, as if they had been separated by great distances – perhaps because when he had left the house that morning she had still taken his presence in her life for granted and now she no longer did.

Going round to the side of the house, she had prayed, 'Please, God, let him be here.' Now she believed that she had felt his nearness through the walls. She had not yet begun to question God's existence, or how he measured up to the images created by her earliest ancestors. But the faith was not in her bones. She did not, as a true believer would have done, now give thanks to him. Emotionally she was still such a child that as soon as she had got what she wanted all else ceased to matter. With 'Papa! Papa!' – mouthing the word because she had spent her breath – she cleaved a path for herself through the standing crowd. Perhaps he was not its centre but for her, where he was always marked the centre of the world.

She laid hold of his arm, claiming possession; she felt for his hand. She would have known it in the dark by its feel: large and strong and unyielding, with hair on the back. The fingertips, the nails on the left were yellow and even his right hand smelled of tobacco. (Selma, washing the net curtains which screened the sitting-room from the street, summoned her daughters to look at the discoloured water and told them, 'That is the colour of your father's lungs.')

Achievement making her arrogant, she interrupted whoever was speaking to ask, 'Why weren't you here before, why didn't you come where you said you would, where have you been?' If those who heard this exchanged smiles, she was unaware of it. She could not afterwards have said who else was there – and some of the men must have been known to her. She had eyes only for her father; it was as if she believed that her looking at him made him be there, as light makes colour.

He did not want her to know what danger he was in, what danger all Jewish men were in on that day; he would rather she thought him irresponsible and inconsiderate, which she did. After questioning him she felt ashamed of herself for having (she believed) shamed him in front of others. 'Go back to your mother,' he said, with less compunction than anyone else who on that day had sent her out into the streets alone. He still believed in the Germany for which he had suffered the Western Front and been willing to die. 'Tell her to meet me at the Mühlfelders' at six o'clock.'

Kate did not know who they were or where they lived. Her mother would know, he told her, returning her to the condition of children to whom adults are giants.

Her hunger for seeing her father sated, but leaving her feeling dissatisfied, she started out again, now beset with anxieties for her mother. What was the good of having found him as long as her mother did not know of it? It made it seem as if his survival mattered to her less than hers – it did so only because his was for the moment assured, but she did not think of that. She was like a juggler keeping two objects airborne at opposite ends of the stage, moving quickly from the one to the other to avert a catastrophe. As if she were fate itself.

In Tante Hete's house, she had had breath enough only because she had not needed much. As soon as she tried to start running again her body failed her. There was a tram at the stop in the Kesselbrink and she jumped on to it, thinking, at least I won't be able to blame myself for not having tried. It was almost empty and she sat down just inside the door, to be able to get away if anyone challenged her. In the state she was in, she would not have hesitated to jump from a tram moving at full speed. Doing away with a Jew had a lot to be said for it.

184

The tram stood and waited. She did not dare to ask the conductor when it would start. She thought of getting off again but did no more than think about it. Other people got on; she was sitting where they all needed to pass her. She had been told often enough to believe it that she did not look Jewish. It ought to have felt to her like a small victory, that she was demonstrating that not every Jew was recognizably different. But she could not point it out to the Aryans about her, and what did a Jew's opinion about Jews matter? She was much more concerned with willing the tram to start.

When it did, it carried her out of her way, as she had known it would, alongside the avenue of elms which led from the town centre, past the town hall and the theatre – beautiful ancient buildings – to the foot of the castle hill. She looked out of the window at what she would soon be leaving and could not hate it for being part of Germany, could not in her mind prefer her imagined Jerusalem. This was where she belonged, she felt unwillingly but could not help it. This was the place which had mothered and fathered her.

To get to the Mühlfelders' house they had once more to pass what was left of the synagogue. This time they were three: also Lise, collected from Frau Nathan's on the way. She walked in the middle to shield her Jewish nose.

A lot of people had congregated here too. Though it was still daylight, the curtains had been drawn to muffle the sound of the wireless, muffled further by those gathered about the table on which it was standing. It was tuned very low to a foreign station broadcasting in German. Kate could not get near enough to hear until it switched to English, when some lost interest and were willing to move aside. She could not understand one word in ten. Few people there could (the foreign language taught in most German high schools then was French). Someone played with the dial until coming upon another German voice, reporting what had happened that day in Berlin. Reporting what had happened elsewhere that day in Germany and Austria, worse things than any that had happened in Bielefeld; worse things than the Jews living there had believed could happen, even in Nazi Germany; worse things than the listening Bielefelder Jews were willing to believe could have happened.

The broadcast over – the announcer said that they were tuned to Radio Moscow – attention shifted. People turned to talk and turned also because somebody had come in. Selma had moved away from the table and was between Kate and the newcomer when she heard, 'All men and boys between the ages of sixteen and sixty –' Selma fell flat on her back on the floor in a faint.

. . . if they did not emigrate, would be put in concentration camps, was the end of that sentence.

Selma was lifted up and laid on a couch. So many people including Lise crowded around her that Kate remained aloof, disclaiming relationship with a mother who needed tending while her husband's whereabouts were once more not known, while God only knew or only the Nazis knew what, meanwhile, had happened to him.

Selma did not want Kate to know what danger he was still in even though the day was almost over. She did not want her to understand what danger they all were going to be in, that today had been worse for the Jews than yesterday not in degree only but also in kind, and that if tomorrow was worse even only by that much more, then those who died quickly were the more fortunate.

She used to say, 'If war breaks out I shall put my head in the gas oven,' and Kate used to think her weak. Selma and Paul lived through two years of the war before having to put on the yellow star; they wore it for fifteen weeks before their deportation. Paul survived forced labour in the Riga ghetto for more than a year, and Selma survived forced labour, his death, and the ghetto itself, until the autumn of 1944 when, if she shared the majority fate, she was shot in a Latvian forest or gassed in Auschwitz.

Eighteen

It was the worst day for Jews in Germany since the Middle Ages.

Within days, neighbouring countries – England, France, Holland, Denmark – offered to provide temporary visas for children who already had somewhere else to go to, to enable them to leave Germany at once. The thought behind this rescue operation was to spare them hardships. No one yet thought that the lives of Jewish children (and women) were in danger.

Selma, who in the spring had agreed that Lise and Kate should go to the Land of Israel, now said that she did not want them too far away. 'Not across water,' she said. Hearing from Alma Rosenthal that she and her sisters had succeeded in arranging their emigration to Holland made Selma decide to register her two younger daughters for that country. (Anne was already too old for the children's transports.)

Anne's belongings preceded her homecoming. One day, on getting back from town, Selma, Lise, and Kate found them on their doorstep inside a dirtied white duvet cover, fine silk panties and gumboots with caked mud on them all jumbled together. Their first thought was, thank God that we have heard from her before this. They had received a postcard saying that she was staying for a few days in Berlin. But then they began to wonder what had happened on the training-farm in Halbe, to cause her – Anne! – to deal thus with her belongings.

When Kate asked her, after she had come home, Anne said, 'I'll tell you when you're twenty-one.' But by that time, Anne had been dead for a year.

She told Lise that the Nazis had come and made all the young people assemble in the yard. They made them run round and round in a circle while they shot at them, killing one and wounding others. Then they gave them an hour to leave the place.

The group to which Anne belonged had arranged to emigrate together to England. Selma pleaded, 'At least let me have the three of you all in one country!' Seventeen years of Anne had taught her the uselessness of arguing with her.

The man responsible for registering the Bielefeld children whose parents wished them to join the transports was Hans Meyer. At the beginning of the year, when Paul had suffered a heart attack, Hans had been given his job as bookkeeper to the Jewish community; he had been allowed to keep it – though there were those who said that he shouldn't – after Paul had recovered: Paul was known to have other sources of income and Hans also had a family to support, and he had been in a concentration camp. According to Selma, Hans felt that he owed them a favour. He also wanted Lise and Kate out of the way to increase his chances of holding on to Paul's job.

When Anne came home, Selma went back to him and asked him to transfer her daughters' names from the list of children going to Holland to that of those going to England. She was only just in time: he was about to take the lists to Berlin for ratification by the central Jewish authorities.

And who were the two children who, most likely unknowingly, were made to exchange places? Did what happened to Horst and Hans-Peter happen to them?

Paul had still been recovering from his heart attack when Kate had come home from Herrlingen for her Easter vacation. The two of them had gone walking: it was said to be good for him, and Kate was made responsible for seeing that he walked neither too fast nor too far – nor stopped at his favourite tobacconist's for a smoke. And still, in the centre of town, at every few steps they encountered someone who lifted his hat to him; at every other street-corner, it seemed to Kate, someone stopped him for a chat. Of course those who knew him at all knew that he was a Jew; if they had not known it while serving with him in the trenches, what had happened to him and his family under the Nazis had made them aware of it. There were at least some to whom this made the difference that they tried to help him.

On the Tenth of November, more than four hundred Jews were arrested in the district of Bielefeld, according to police records. Paul may have been one of them. Somebody told Kate – long after her father's death – that he had once spent a day in prison. Most of the arrested men were taken to Buchenwald, and one of those men was, at the beginning of December, returned in a sealed coffin. With Dr Kronheim still abroad and Friedemann in a concentration camp, Paul was among those who assumed responsibility for the funeral. There was some talk of opening the coffin, to make certain that it contained the remains of Richard Baer and not some make-weight, and to discover why it had been sealed. The death certificate stated that he had died of pneumonia.

That was another thing about which Kate was still too young to be told the full truth.

The father of one of Frau Nathan's assistants was an engine driver; he drove trains with Jews to concentration camps and when Lise returned to work after the Tenth of November she was told about some of the things he spoke of having seen.

But neither Lise nor Anne was allowed to look in the small black tin box in which their father kept his wartime mementoes. Along with Kate, they had to keep to the far end of the long sitting-room table when he opened it to take out his medals, including the Iron Cross, to be worn with top hat and frock coat on special occasions, on the High Holy Days for instance, when it was he who was chosen to ascend, together with Dr Kronheim and Friedemann, to the ark, to receive the extra torah scroll which was then taken out. According to Selma, the honour was bestowed upon him in memory of her father; Kate preferred to believe that he was chosen because of all the men he looked the most splendid.

He did not talk about his experiences in the trenches except in his sleep. Twenty years after the end of the war – to the end of his life, probably, even in the Riga ghetto – he suffered nightmares from which he woke shouting for help.

From as far back as Kate could remember, her father had to be shown special consideration, to have allowances made for him because of what he had suffered during the war. Quite unpredictably, sometimes, in the course of a meal for instance, a thoughtless remark by one of his daughters would trigger off a string of swear-words and his fist would come down with such force that the things on the table danced.

Men who were strangers to Kate also showed him special consideration, sometimes when this was needed most. If he was among those who were rounded up to supply the quota of four hundred Jews demanded from the district of Bielefeld, then someone must have intervened on his behalf. His wartime record should have protected him and Selma from being on that first transport to the east, should have ensured that they were allowed to remain where they were until May 1943, and that then they were sent to Theresienstadt, where conditions were less terrible and could, with luck, be survived.

They were not on the original list which the Gestapo tendered to the Jewish community. But a married couple whose names were on it attempted to gas themselves. They were found in time to be revived, and sent with a later transport to Auschwitz from where they did not return. They were unfit to travel and the Jewish community needed to find substitutes. Someone working in its offices must have said, 'How about Paul and Selma Loewenthal, their daughters are no longer here, there's just the two of them.' Long afterwards Kate saw the Gestapo list: the typewritten names of Julius and Jenni Hesse had pencil lines through them, and her parents' names had been added in pencil in the small space between the last typewritten line and the Gestapo official's signature.

Though they were leaving home for England, Lise and Kate gave no thought to living in that country. They were not, at the cost of being separated from their parents and losing their mother-tongue and leaving their native town, going to settle in another place where people would sooner or later say to them, Jews go home. They had been preparing themselves for years and now prepared their luggage to go to the Land of Israel. They were allowed to take with them only as much as they could carry.

In late November and early December they went about Bielefeld – walking in the gutter, passing shops *verboten* to Jews – to buy straw hats and shorts; Youth Aliyah had provided them with a list of what to bring. Alsberg on the Jahnplatz had been Aryanized; but the non-Jewish staff remained the same and some of them remembered the *Frau Architekt* from when she had had more money to spend than they would earn in a year. Selma always treated those who served her with consideration, and was repaid with devotion: the cotton summer frocks were brought out of storage for Lise and Kate to try on and buy a couple each. Selma was not going to send her daughters out into the world as if they were beggars though that was what they were; Paul had borrowed the necessary money. But it was not even enough to buy them serviceable suitcases: by the time they got to Dortmund, where they had to change trains, one side of the handle on Kate's came undone.

For years they had traded heaps of their old toys for half a handful of things more suitable to their age. Now they sold most of their books. Kate bought herself a pocket-knife and a leather belt, and two rolls of film for her camera. Half a mark was all the cash they were allowed to take out of Germany. In England, too, they would be depending on charity and there it would have to come from strangers.

The books which the government had banned, for instance, Gorki's *Mother*, which was one of Kate's favourite books just then, they tore up and fed into the kitchen stove. Kate owned a small thin volume of reproductions of Jacob Steinhardt's woodcuts of ghetto scenes, which she packed among her clothes without Selma's knowledge; it was to cause her a bad moment at the frontier, when a German customs official examined her case. Had it been found it would have been confiscated, but nothing worse would have happened. The Germans were dumping what Jews they could on the rest of the world and the truth is that the rest of the world did not want them either. Two years, their entry visas said, Lise and Kate would be allowed to remain in England – or until they reached the age of seventeen. When Lise reached that age, two months before war broke out, she was made to move on.

There were other belongings which Kate felt she could not bear to part from but she did. She asked her mother to keep them for her until she came back – and was too caught up in the present to speculate when that might be. Until quite recently, Kate had still

191

been buying herself toys, cuddly animals mostly; even Lise had only the previous year spent all her savings on a doll that was very like a baby, one of the first of its kind. Their mother disapproved of them wasting their money like that but could not stop them; her disapproval stopped them only from enjoying what they had bought.

Yet Kate valued none of her things as much as the least thing belonging to Anne. In the days following the *Kristallnacht*, every morning when Selma and Lise and she left the flat – Anne was still in Berlin – Kate filled her pockets from Anne's untouchable collection of wooden animal ornaments. She chose all the family groups: a nest of robins, a cat with kittens; they must have appealed to her as talismans. She took them because she feared that something would happen to the flat in their absence which would prevent them from ever returning to it. But not even the windows facing the street were broken. The only trespasser was Herr Haupt, who owned the corner shop where they owed a lot of money; he left a cardboard box full of groceries on their balcony.

After the Tenth of November, Kate was convinced that her father had friends enough not to be physically harmed. If Jewish women were physically harmed on that day – in places like Bielefeld – it was by their own hand or accidentally. The only Jewish women to be put into concentration camps at that time were those who were politically active: communists. Nobody told Kate that the worst was not yet over. Her parents did not tell her that they expected worse to come. They did not tell her, we are loath to let you go because of the possibility that we may never see each other again. On the contrary, to make the parting easier for the child they connived in pretending that it was not different in kind, that she was merely going further away, as she had been doing every time since first leaving home at the age of eleven to go to Salzuflen. This time she was going across the water and wasn't it an adventure? Of course the thought of it was, to Kate.

If there were moments (there were) when her mother behaved as if she believed that this was the final parting, Kate saw them as manifestations of her mother's excessive emotionalism – or that was how she interpreted her mother's response to the world they lived in. Kate was reaching, had reached, the stage of adolescent rebellion against her mother while idolizing her father and, because it was so when she left, this was how it remained, her feelings towards them frozen at the moment of leaving.

One day early in December their mother said to Lise and Kate, 'Come with me one more time to Opa's and Oma's grave.' In Bielefeld there were many cemeteries that were laid out like parkland; at the end of the number 1 tramline for instance, beyond Brackwede, lay the Senne Cemetery, which was as popular for staid Sunday family excursions as the small zoo of indigenous animals was with families in which the children were brought up less strictly.

Selma often went into the small cemetery opposite the synagogue in Turner Street when she was in town and wanted to rest her legs; it was only a few steps from the Jahnplatz. Even after the *Kristallnacht*, a Christian cemetery was a public place in which a Jew could sit without fear of being molested – at least in Bielefeld. There were four small stone angels over four small graves of siblings who had died young, presumably in some epidemic. Whenever Selma visited this cemetery she contrived to pass there, and would pause long enough to need to dry her eyes.

Sentimental old cow, the teenaged Kate thought.

On that last visit to their Opa's and Oma's grave, after having stood by it for long enough to satisfy convention, Selma said, 'Come, I have something to show you.' And took them no more than perhaps ten paces to the end of that path; it led on to another and a row of children's graves, instantly recognizable as such by the smallness not only of the graves but of the headstones. The one before which she stopped was roof-like, would with more depth have been a miniature house. Her fat constrained by her corset, she bent down to smooth away, with her soft warm delicate white fingers, the ivy leaves from the inscription which read, *Knabe* Loewenthal: here lay her firstborn, a boy baby who had not lived long enough to be given a name.

In all the years of Lise's and Kate's childhood she had not mentioned him. She had told them lies about her earliest years of marriage, saying that when she and Paul had lived in two rooms in Roon Street and had been given notice when her pregnancy began to show, that had been the beginning of the problems caused her by Anne.

Saying that whenever she had come back from her search for a self-contained flat – eventually finding the one in Roland Street – the landlady had been hovering in wait for her, and that this had conditioned Anne in the womb to dislike the moment of homecoming. Calling Anne, and referring to her, as her first-born.

Why?

And what other lies had she told them which, given time, she would one day have had to admit to in order to tell them the truth?

And why tell them now – what difference could it possibly make to them, going to the Land of Israel (or at least England), to know that with greater luck or less adversity or a more benevolent God they would have been blessed with an older brother? What possible difference could it make to her, their knowing this before they went away? There was little enough to tell about that baby. Was she not rather telling them something about herself?

Was it perhaps not her greatest, but her only secret, and was telling it to them meant to be her parting gift?

After their names had been put down for England on the Thursday – four weeks after the *Kristallnacht* – they were told that they would be leaving on the following Wednesday. It made Kate happy to learn that their waiting time had been cut down. 'Wednesday, tra-la-la,' she went about singing. Wednesday had always been her lucky day.

On her last Friday evening in Germany, she went to attend the service held on the ground floor of the community rooms, which was without windows but otherwise undamaged. It was packed with men in their dark winter coats; there were no women and no other children. Only the most orthodox had come, men whose faces she had not seen before or had not noticed, praying not as a congregation but each for himself and wandering about, communicating by raising their voices in prayer as they exchanged meaningful looks. They took care not to come too close to her for fear of touching her accidentally, as if she were a plague-carrier or as if she were wearing an invisible halo. She had meant to give thanks to God but was constantly distracted by thinking, I shouldn't have come, and baffled that in the midst of Jews she could feel such an outsider, so alone.

On their last day in Germany, Lise and Kate got up before it was morning. Anne had allowed the curtain to remain open all night and she called to them while they were still in some make-do pyjamas to come and kiss her goodbye so that she could go back to sleep; they expected to see each other again before long in England. They had looked at England on the map of the world and thought it very small, small enough for Anne still to be almost together with Lise and Kate once she came. That was just one of their many expectations in which reality was to prove them wrong.

All the everyday routine things they did that morning they were doing for the last time at home. Kate did not think of this for thinking with a blissful heart, as if she were in possession of assurances about her future, by tomorrow we shall be in England. Her impatience had cut grooves in her character which made her pay attention to what was coming only when it had come.

Perhaps she was incapable of thinking of the moment because all her faculties were required to cope with it, she found living so difficult. In theory she took thought. Returning from Rüdnitz, she had expected their mother to be at the station to meet them because this was the last time – for the foreseeable future – they would be arriving in Bielefeld. That was a consideration she could cope with. Though she loved the town as much as it was in her nature to love a place – and that was passionately – it had, like Ingrid Modersohn, failed to reciprocate her love. If in that final hour with her parents there had come to her the thought, this is the last time I am leaving home – perhaps she could not have made herself do it, would have cried, screamed, clung to the doorpost, run back in and fought off anyone who tried to make her leave and not listened to anything anyone might have said. She had not loved her home, had not been aware of loving it while she had it. She did know that it was the only home she had and that whatever home the future would provide her with would be no more than a substitute, a second best.

It was still dark enough when they left the house for even the smaller stars to be visible in the sky above their neighbourhood on the edge of the town, which cast its own rosily orange glow. The air was still and frosty. Before they had walked as far as the *Stürmer* box at the corner of the main road, the night was beginning to fade.

They were walking loudly, the only people out in the street at that hour, though here and there, behind curtains, lights were being switched on. They were walking so loudly that they did not dare to speak. Also, they had nothing left to say, or rather what they had to say could not be said, was better left unsaid, could not have expressed what they felt and even so would have been too much to put into words too hurtful to hear. Out of habit and out of defiance they walked on the pavement, and not because there was no one about; they continued to use the pavement also on the main road.

Here, at the tram stops, clusters of workmen were waiting for the earliest tram. They looked at the family approaching and walking past them, perhaps only because it provided something to look at. Kate, impatient with their parents' reluctant pace, was drawing ahead and Lise was keeping beside her; each was carrying her own suitcase, because – was their leaving not proof of it? – by now they had grown more capable than their parents.

At the tram stop by the gasworks, where the road ascended, a man stepped out of the group to block their way. He said, 'Allow me to carry your suitcases.'

They did not know what to make of his offer; it frightened them just as much as if he had threatened them. Their chief concern was that they should not cause their father to get into trouble; to avoid this they were prepared to do anything, even jeopardize their departure. They were not old enough to hold on to the distinction which the Nazis had done away with. As for the Nazis there were no good Jews, for these children there were at that moment no good Germans.

They remained standing like that, the man blocking the girls' way – they tried moving off the pavement and he moved with them – until their parents caught up. To them he said loudly, within the hearing of all who were at that tram stop, 'I want you to know that not every German agrees with what is being done in our name to you Jews.'

Then he stood aside. But he called after them, 'I want your daughters to remember this!'

Perhaps the station was not as busy as it seemed to Kate, only seemed busy to her because she had not expected anyone else to be there, not only because of the early hour, but because what she and Lise were doing was so important to them that she had expected the station to look as if it existed only for their departure. It was full of people who were nothing to do with it.

There were other children, other parents; not many but some. Identifiable by each family unit keeping tightly together and by the expression on the faces: grief on those of the adults and on the children's, excitement tempered by doubt. Some had come, presumably the evening before, from neighbouring places, to catch this train which already had other children on board and three reserved compartments and would, in Dortmund, connect with the Berlin express, with whole carriages reserved for the three hundred children making up this second transport.

At the time of the first transport, twelve days before, the boarding in Bielefeld had occasioned scenes talked about at the station that morning in hushed voices. This time there were Brownshirts as well as policemen and station personnel to keep order.

The separation from their mother came before they expected it; this time parents were not allowed on to the platform. It happened for Kate more hastily than she had foreseen. As always, the train arrived minutes before its departure time and was announced minutes before its arrival. The announcement came – summoning her! – while she was still on the wrong side of the barrier. Her mother was holding her, holding on to her, holding her back.

She had put her suitcase down so as to have her hands free to hug her mother – because it was expected of her and not because she felt like it. If she had at that moment felt anything she could not have left her mother. Though she did not know that she was leaving her for ever (that thought did not even occur to her), this was the first time she was leaving home without knowing when she would be coming back.

To cut short the Jewish leave-taking, or merely being efficient, someone picked up her suitcase and passed it across the barrier where someone who stood there accepted it and put it down.

All her belongings! In later life she was not materialistic. Perhaps she was as a child – she was made to believe that she was, because she liked eating and because she always wanted what her sisters and especially Anne had. She valued excessively at that moment her shoddy suitcase with the clothes she would soon wear out and other things – none of them irreplaceable – probably only because they stood for home, the only part of home, beside Lise, she was taking away with her. She left her mother to rush after it.

And when she looked back there was Lise, still being with their mother, finding it harder than Kate to leave her, making Kate understand that she had failed to find it hard enough. The barrier, other children coming through it, and the men who were there to keep order, all made it too late for her to go back to her mother so that she could part from her in the way she ought to have done.

Her father, still able at that time somehow to fix things so that it looked as if he, like Anne, were not to be counted among those who were victims, had been allowed to go ahead in order to help see the children on to the train. It meant that he remained within sight of Lise and Kate a little longer, but without being available to them: he was the only Jewish father on the platform and all the departing children were competing for his attention. It was like Paul, to be unaware of how much his daughters needed him just then.

Immediately after the train drew out of the station, there was, on the right, the Jewish cemetery. Then, on the left, there came that symbol of Bielefeld, the Sparrenburg castle. But before the castle there was the Oetker custard powder factory. The smell of it, a smell that belonged to their childhood, remained with them until all the familiar landmarks – Brackwede, the forest, the heath – had been left behind.

(*L to R*) Lise, Kate, Anne, with Selma, on the beach